ETCs
New Methods for
U.S. Exporting

Leo G. B. Welt, Editor

AMA Management Briefing

AMA MEMBERSHIP PUBLICATIONS DIVISION
AMERICAN MANAGEMENT ASSOCIATIONS

Library of Congress Cataloging in Publication Data
Main entry under title:

ETCs, new methods for U.S. exporting.

(AMA management briefing)
1. Export trading companies—Law and legislation—
United States.   2. Export trading companies—United
States.   I. Welt, Leo G. B., 1934-   II. Title:
E.T.C.s, new methods for U.S. exporting.   III. Title:
ETCs, new methods for United States exporting.
IV. Title: ETCs, new methods for US exporting,
V. Series.
KF1988.E83   1983   343.73'0878   83-22487
ISBN 0-8144-2300-0   347.303878

*This Management Briefing has been distributed to all members enrolled in the
International Division of the American Management Associations. Copies may
be purchased at the following single-copy rates: AMA members, $7.50. Non-
members, $10.00. Students, $3.75 (upon presentation of a college/university
identification card at an AMA bookstore). Faculty members may purchase 25
or more copies for classroom use at the student discount rate (order on college
letterhead).*

First Printing

Contents

Leo G. B. Welt

Introduction

The Export Trading Company Act (ETCA) of 1982 rode on the wave of some exceptionally optimistic expectations. Proponents of the legislation saw it as a major catalyst in spurring U.S exports, vis-à-vis the rest of the trading world, to the levels they were only a decade ago. An increase in trading company activity, some said, could create between 340,000 and 640,000 jobs within three to four years and boost the U.S. GNP by $27 to $55 billion by 1985.

What can we say about these early expectations—given a one-year perspective on the legislation?

Without question, the ETCA has raised the export awareness of American business leaders. By eliminating many of the uncertainties that, in the past, posed as obstacles to exporting, and by bringing together various vital elements needed to coordinate effective trading companies, the act could be extremely successful in reducing the overall U.S. trade deficit. The current high level of interest in exporting, coupled with a healthy dose of American creativity, put this goal within reach.

Although some of the developments of the past year have gone against the grain of the legislation's original intentions, the groundwork is now being laid for a surge in export activity.

ABOUT THE AUTHOR

Leo G. B. Welt is president of Welt International Corp., a Washington, D.C.-based export trading company. Prior to establishing Welt International in 1967, he conducted international trade in management positions for International Paper, Weyerhauser Co., and Miehle-Goss Dexter.

Mr. Welt has written two books, *Countertrade: Business Practices for Today's World Market* and *Trade Without Money*, and his articles have appeared in the *New York Times,* the *Washington Post,* and *Business America.* He is publisher and editor-in-chief of a number of international newsletters, including *China Business and Trade* and *East/West Technology Digest.*

He provided active support for the passage of the Export Trading Company Act of 1982, and he continues to advise financial and industrial corporations that are establishing their own ETCs.

A native of Berlin, Mr. Welt was graduated from Princeton University.

QUESTIONS OF LARGE AND SMALL

The purpose of the Export Trading Company Act is to encourage U.S. exports by facilitating the formation of U.S. export trading companies to provide international sales and support services for small- and medium-sized domestic producers. The Department of Commerce estimates that up to 20,000 U.S. manufacturers now offer goods and services that could be highly competitive abroad. Yet, the small size and inexperience of these manufacturing firms leave them ill-equipped to absorb the front-end costs and risks involved in developing overseas markets.

The ETCA not only permits banking institutions to own equity in export trading companies, but also encourages various combinations of other services. Banks, freight forwarders, export management companies, manufacturers, and governmental bodies can join together to provide a variety of services—consulting, international market research, advertising, marketing, transportation (including documentation and freight forwarding), communication, foreign exchange, and financing. Offered to small- and medium-sized manufacturers, these services could reduce the overall risk and ease the financial burden to the point that many firms that have not exported in the past can now do so.

In theory, then, the ETCA was drafted to elicit interest and involvement from smaller manufacturers in exporting. An intensive lobbying campaign directed the legislation to this segment of the manufacturing community and cleared the way for easy passage of the act. *To date, the act has not proved effective in spurring small business exports.* What we are witnessing today is a great deal of activity by the larger multinationals to take advantage of certain provisions (also inserted after an intense lobbying effort) contained, primarily, in Title II, the Bank Export Services Act of 1982.

Large banks are currently seeking manufacturing firms and trading companies with an established background in international trade as a prerequisite for ETC participation. Therefore, rather than providing new opportunities for smaller firms, the ETCA is primarily helping existing multinationals by promoting the formation of larger trading companies. These companies may, in turn, adapt their infrastructures to carry product lines offered by smaller U.S. producers.

ABOUT THIS BRIEFING

The movement by the multinationals to take advantage of the Act is, by no means, cause for criticism. It may mean nothing more than that the smaller firms have yet to learn how to put all of the elements vital to exporting together into an effective organization, or how to find their way through the bureaucratic processes needed for certification.

By providing information from leading authorities in law, finance, government, and business, this publication intends to add to the growing body of knowledge needed to make the ETCA work—for companies of all sizes. First, however, a look at the major provisions of the act, at the flexibility this legislation provides, and at the factors that will be critical to the success of American-style ETCs.

ETCs: New Methods for U.S. Exporting—7

TITLE I: EXPORT TRADING COMPANY ACT OF 1982

The Export Trading Company Act of 1982 contains within it four separate titles. Title I provides the definition of an Export Trading Company, as follows:

> Any profit or nonprofit organization doing business under the laws of the United States or any state which is organized and operated principally for the purpose of either (a) exporting goods or services produced in the U.S. for its members, or (b) by providing one or more export trading services, facilitating the exportation of goods and services produced in the U.S. by unaffiliated persons.

This definition is much broader than that of a Webb-Pomerene Association because it also includes the export of services. This definition also allows an ETC to be engaged *principally*, rather than *exclusively*, in exporting, and it provides the flexibility needed to engage in activities such as countertrade, third-party trade, and importing. Title I also provides for the establishment of an office within the Department of Commerce having specific responsibility for facilitating the development of ETCs and administering the antitrust certificate of review.

TITLE II: BANK EXPORT SERVICES ACT OF 1982

By encouraging bank investment and involvement in ETCs, this Title departs, substantially, from the long-standing policy of separating banking and commerce. Congress has attempted to encourage exports through bank investment, while simultaneously minimizing the risk. The title not only imposes strict limitations on both the amount of money a bank can invest in and the amount of credit it can extend to an ETC, but also requires the regulatory presence of the Federal Reserve Board. The board must give its approval before a banking institution can proceed with its ETC operations, whether they be in the form of a joint venture or organized as a direct subsidiary of the bank.

The ETCA restricts bank investment in ETCs to bank holding companies, banker's banks, and Edge Act corporations. The amount of any such investment is limited to 5 percent of the holding company's consolidated capital and surplus. An Edge Act corporation not engaged in banking is limited to 25 percent of its consolidated capital and surplus.

To protect the role of banks as impartial arbiters of credit, the ETCA limits loans to ETCs to 10 percent of the bank holding company's consolidated capital and surplus. Also included under Title II are various provisions directing the Export Import Bank and various governmental agencies such as the Small Business Administration to promote small business exports through the establishment of more liberal export financing guidelines. The role of Banker's Acceptances has also been revised and modified to promote greater U.S. exports.

Recently, some U.S. bankers have expressed concern over the position the Federal Reserve Board has taken in disallowing banks to organize for the exportation of their own banking services. A bank might find it advantageous, for example, to package its present international services and form a trading company that would sell these amalgamated service packages to smaller exporters for a specified fee. The bank would use its overseas networks, financial resources, and international marketing services to facilitate the role of a "one stop" trading house.

Although this right clearly exists under the ETCA, and was specifically intended by Congress, the FRB ruling effectively prohibits U.S. banks from carrying out such operations. Many feel that the ruling is an outright misinterpretation, while others believe that it is only temporary and should be taken as nothing more than an indication of the FRB's cautious attitude. Whatever the case, the issues are still not resolved. Chapters 5 and 6 provide more perspective.

TITLE III: CERTIFICATE OF REVIEW

The antitrust certification procedure set forth in Title III attempts to provide a balance between encouraging exports and preventing violation of federal antitrust laws. The purpose of the Certificate of Review is to provide exporters with the assurance that their export operations will be immune from antitrust challenge. In addition, it dissuades private annoyance suits by charging the plaintiff in such a suit with the payment of the attorneys' fees, should the plaintiff lose in litigation. Also, it reduces the defendant's liability from treble to single damages in the event that the plaintiff does win his case.

Under Title III, only those export trading companies that feel that their export-related activities may somehow violate U.S. federal or state laws need apply to the Office of Export Trading Company Affairs within the Department of Commerce for an antitrust Certificate of Review. Should the application for such a certificate be approved by the Department of Commerce and, in turn, have the concurrence of the Justice Department, the holder is protected from U.S. government antitrust action, providing that the holder operates within the constraints set forth within the certificate.

Banks, on the other hand, are required to seek approval from the Federal Reserve Board for their proposed activities, as specified under Title II. The FRB has 60 days from the time the application is submitted to deny such proposed activities. Should the FRB take no action within 60 days, the bank is free to enter into its proposed ETC investment.

As of September 1983, approximately 160 export trading companies had been formed within the U.S., according to an estimate provided by the Department of Commerce. Most of these companies have not found it necessary to obtain the antitrust protection offered by the Certificate of Review.

The certificate is not a prerequisite for forming an ETC, and, in fact, it is being utilized by only a handful of companies. Many U.S. firms have acted as trading companies for years, and they can continue to do so, providing that they take appropriate legal safeguards. ETCs are encouraged to seek the certificate, should they feel that some part of their activities may raise antitrust issues. For most firms, however, the practice has been to rely on the advice of their counsel to guide them away from possible future litigation.

TITLE IV: FOREIGN TRADE ANTITRUST IMPROVEMENTS ACT OF 1982

Title IV amends the Sherman Act and Section 5 of the Federal Trade Commission Act. These amendments clarify that the prior legislation does not apply to export trade unless there is an adverse anticompetitive effect on commerce in the United States or on the export commerce of a U.S. resident.

CRITICAL SUCCESS FACTORS

Since the signing of the Act in October of 1982, various forms of ETCs have developed within the U.S., each tailored to suit the needs of its owners by being either product oriented or totally market oriented. No matter what the driving force behind an ETC, several essential ingredients are common to most.

Cooperation with the manufacturer. Whether the ETC is an extension of a larger multinational selling only its products or those closely related to its product line, or a general trading house dealing with a multitude of product lines, the ETC must have close contact with the actual manufacturer or producer of the products. Although this is apparent for many reasons, two factors—financial support and the need for product modifications—claim the most importance.

For smaller manufacturers engaged in the production of specialty goods, financial support is often critical. Should the ETC prefer to play the role of a broker, it should be in a position close enough to the manufacturer to help arrange credit for the goods being sold through the ETC.

Similarly, there are many instances in which slight product modifications, achieved at a relatively low cost to the manufacturer, have greatly enhanced the appeal of the product in different foreign markets. With the market research provided by the foreign representatives of the ETC, it is very easy for many U.S. goods to be modified in order to compete directly with goods already produced in those countries.

Extensive use of market research is critical for other reasons as well. Without reliable data on foreign markets, it would be impossible for any ETC to direct its product lines (and those of others which it is carrying) toward appropriate foreign markets and to establish effective tactics for selling the products in those markets. In the past, the major problem in using such market research has been the relative unreliability of the data. As the success of some of the larger foreign trading companies reveals, reliable market research enables a company to service the right markets, with the appropriate goods, at the right time. Most major trading companies have contacts in all major markets, and these contacts relay market trends, in terms of basic demand and product need, back to the home office. For any U.S. ETC to become successful, it also must establish and support an extensive network of foreign contacts.

Knowledge and experience in the physical processes of international trade. This includes knowing how to identify the purchaser's needs, how to make the deal, and how to arrange credit terms, insurance, documentation, and physical delivery, among other factors. The ETC should either control or have clear access to a domestic infrastructure for handling these processes: domestic offices, domestic transportation systems, access to ports, freight forwarding and insurance, export documentation, shipping, and communications. Although there is no need to own these outright, the trading company should have preferential access to at least some of these facilities and services.

Expertise in foreign currency. With fluctuating exchange rates, the ability to properly hedge foreign currencies could be crucial to the trading company's success. Knowing how to deal in the purchasing country's currency and when and how to use third-country currencies is also vital.

A vast amount of financial backing. Along with the need for financing comes the need for the international financial contacts that grow out of the trading company's association with large multinational financial institutions. Unless the trading company is a direct extension of a larger multinational firm, one that can provide many of the financial services itself, the trading company must work closely with an international bank. Two main financial factors are involved: the financial strength to back a fairly substantial network of operations, and the ability to extend credit. The latter requires not only control of financial resources, but also the institutional background and mechanisms needed to be an effective credit lending entity.

A large trading company should be in the position to extend credit to both domestic manufacturers and foreign purchasers. Should the ETC take title to the goods which it trades, it should be able to finance both the purchasing of the products and the warehousing of the inventories. The older foreign trading companies often work with a capital-to-sales ratio of 1 to 20, and they are able to operate on extremely small profit ratios, often less than 1 percent. In contrast, many U.S. export management companies have difficulty in reaching a capital-to-sales ratio of 1 to 6. For this reason alone, a U.S. trading company modeled after the foreign concept would require vast amounts of operating capital.

ETCs: THE AMERICAN CONCEPT

The definition of an export trading company under Title I of the ETCA was intended to provide the flexibility needed to adapt the concept to a wide range of U.S. manufacturing and service industries. Title I type ETCs were already in existence as of the signing date of the Act. They were not called export trading companies. However, they did provide many, if not all, of the same services described in the ETC legislation. Such examples are export management companies, freight forwarders, commodity-focused associations, and Webb-Pomerene Associations.

There is no specific model for how the trading company should be structured. However, four service elements will normally be present: market development, sales and distribution, customer service, and financial service. These make up the trading company's core service package, and activities in the respective areas may be summarized as follows:

Market Development
1. Keeping abreast of foreign market conditions and potential.
2. Developing and meeting product needs in foreign markets.
3. Identifying U.S. products that are likely to sell in specific foreign markets.
4. Conducting research and analysis of overseas markets.
5. Conducting country-by-country product feasibility studies.
6. Providing market entry assistance.

Sales and Distribution
1. Assuming all export responsibilities.
2. Managing the foreign sales network.

3. Providing administrative services for import controls, customer clearance, tariffs, freight, and insurance.
4. Arranging for all inventory warehousing.
5. Acting as representative or distributor securing goods from U.S. processors to meet orders.

Financial Package
1. Obtaining credit information, including an assessment of credit-worthiness of foreign customers.
2. Risk assessment and analysis.
3. Re-invoicing merchandise and submitting same in local currency after including all expenses.
4. Managing collections, payments, and foreign exchange.
5. Arranging for local currency financing.

Customer Service
1. Developing and maintaining contact with major customers abroad.
2. Establishing in-country distributors.
3. Arranging in-country service networks.
4. Organizing customer service networks.
5. Managing customer relations and distributor relations.

It may be presumed that economies of scale will favor larger ETCs having extensive information and contact networks overseas. At the same time, there are also many opportunities for smaller ETCs to emerge with an appropriate marketing concept and a specialty product.

One such model is that of a specialized trading company. This company would concentrate on selling one product to a particular country or region. These firms would tend to be smaller, and their products might well require sophisticated marketing and promotional activities. Such an ETC could be designed locally: a Mississippi-based ETC dealing only with poultry or catfish, for example. Or it might be project oriented: an ETC dealing only in cattle, for example. A locally based ETC, such as the one mentioned above, would contain within it producers of poultry or catfish, a local bank, a shipping company, and a packing plant. A product-oriented ETC would include cattle producers from various states rather than just one localized area.

The concept of a regional trading company provides another possible ETC model. This ETC would concentrate on products produced in the region, both commodities and processed goods. This model would be primarily focused on exports and should have under its control the entire core service package. A Georgia-based company, for example, might deal in poultry, wood products, peaches, and pecans. It would include the producers, a shipping company, a bank holding company, an export management company, a port authority, and a state economic development authority.

An extension of this previous model would be an ETC designed around a local port authority. This ETC would deal in locally accessible goods that could be shipped from the local port. Any such venture would require the backing of a governmental body to aid in its initial development and financing. The port authority ETC would then coordinate and direct the various other units involved in the ETC, such as the export management company, producers, shippers, banks, and governmental economic development agencies.

Another, more popular ETC model is that offered under the direction of a multinational corporation. With the help of outside financing (something not always necessary), the multinational would use its own in-house departments to coordinate both importing and exporting services. Since many multinationals already have extensive overseas networks of either buyers or sellers in place, the ETC would reverse the flow and trade both ways through their pre-established networks. Most of the ETC's core service package would already be in existence; thus, little effort in adding on new services would be necessary. In addition, the multinational could adapt to carry smaller competitors' product lines overseas. This would greatly diversify the array of products offered by the ETC.

One other model might develop: a full-scale trading company, fashioned after the larger European and Japanese trading companies. As an American alternative, such a trading company would be rare, because of the large scale on which such an ETC would have to operate. Rather than being product driven, as most of the previously mentioned models would be, this ETC would be completely market driven. The company would be transnational in its operation and would enter any market from which a profit could be derived. The majority of the service core package would be contained in-house, with strong financial backing being offered in order to take advantage of short-term market shortages throughout the world.

With American trading firms entering this dynamic area of international trade at a relatively late point in time, one can expect an array of creative ETC models to develop over the next few years. Already, since the signing of the Act into law in October of 1982, many of the larger U.S. multinational firms have either taken steps toward the actual formation of an ETC, or are about to do so. The next few years will be vital to the development of the U.S. economy, in general, and to export trade, in particular.

1

David A. Field

ETCs—The Activity to Date*

Since October of 1982, various companies have made public their intentions to proceed with the establishment of export trading companies, while countless others have seriously considered what benefits such a trading entity would provide in the foreign marketplace. The legislation, then, is taking hold. And many of the companies now forming offer unique examples of how ETCs can be organized.

In the case of the joint venture between Sears World Trade, Inc., a subsidiary of Sears Roebuck and Company, and First Chicago Corporation, the distinctiveness will come through a powerful overseas network, developed at a shared cost of $35 million. A modification and expansion of the already extensive Sears network grafted to the overseas network provided by The First Chicago Corporation (one of the largest in the world, with 62 offices in 33 countries) means that the new company will be in a position to offer its clients a complete array of exporting services. Sears World Trade, Inc., will concentrate on marketing consumer goods and light industrial equipment worldwide, draw-

*The views expressed in this chapter are those of the author and not necessarily those of the Office of Export Trading Company Affairs.

ETCs: New Methods for U.S. Exporting—17

ABOUT THE AUTHOR

David A. Field is currently employed by the Department of Commerce—Office of Export Trading Company Affairs, where he is actively involved with strategic and antitrust issues affecting the formation of ETCs. He holds a bachelors degree in business administration from Western Michigan University.

ing from the traditional suppliers of Sears Roebuck and Company. It will specialize in sales of technology and management services, export sales, import sales, third-country trade (cross trading), and countertrade arrangements. Because of the high rate of projected growth in the Pacific Basin countries, Sears World Trade will focus much of its efforts on that area.

Other major ETC ventures—Control Data Commerce International, K-Mart Trading Services International, General Electric, and Burlington Northern International, to name a few—were established primarily to expand their parent companys' respective international divisions. Most are adapting to carry competitors' products in addition to their own, with the hope of broadening their overall coverage of foreign markets. Control Data Commerce International, for example, has targeted potential markets for technical business, technical medical and dental products, and commercial energy management. This company also plans to be available as a source of information and contacts for small- to medium-sized firms. Burlington Northern International hopes to provide valuable contacts for smaller firms, concentrating on dealing in logs, lumber, and (possibly) coal. K-Mart Trading Services International, another example, is attempting to utilize its extensive foreign buyers network and modify the current process to use its overseas contacts to sell U.S. goods abroad. K-Mart recently made public its intention to work with U.S. manufacturers who wish to use K-Mart's trade services for exporting the products of smaller manufacturing firms.

Because of the flexible definition of what an export trading company should be or do, a variety of ETC models are developing. (Keep in mind only bank-affiliated ETCs must derive 51 percent of their income from exporting.) Many of the ETCs mentioned are doing little to expand their present infrastructure. Instead, they are modifying their networks to adapt to the exporting of extensive product lines. Companies that were primarily importers of foreign goods (such as K-Mart) are now using their networks to export as well as import. On the other hand, firms that primarily exported in the past are now adapting to include some importing and countertrade deals. Because of the ETC legislation, then, many large U.S. multinationals are reviewing and altering their present international operations. By providing services to other manufacturers of rebated product lines, they can better service their own foreign markets.

Current developments in the ETC field have not, however, been limited to the larger multinationals. The Export Trading Company Act has spurred much interest from many smaller- and medium-sized manufacturers and suppliers who feel that the legislation has finally opened the door for their exports. Leading the way in this area are many of the larger export management firms. In the past, these firms have been severely limited by lack of financial strength and insufficient exposure to producers. Currently, because of the opportunity for bank involvement with ETCs, coupled with the increased export awareness brought by the Act, these export management companies are expanding to diversify their product lines and extend their present exporting services.

Under the Export Trading Company Act, governmental bodies are allowed to both promote and establish export trading companies—one major factor which will aid in the developing of export markets for smaller U.S. producers. Along with the coordination offered by governmental economic development agencies, such an ETC will combine the essential ETC elements with less difficulty than a local, nongovernment-sponsored venture. ETCs currently under proposal are those established around regional port authorities. One recent example is the New York, New Jersey Port Authority, which has established a "one-stop" trading company called XPORT. XPORT will concentrate its first efforts on facilitating overseas sales of consumer goods and light industrial products from small- and medium-sized manufacturers.

XPORT and other such ETCs are developed by tying together an export management company, a freight forwarder, a financial institution, and various area manufacturers, all on a regional basis. These ETCs will not be product-specific trading firms, but will instead cater to the exporting needs of the surrounding producers. Because many of these port authorities already offer a package of exporting services, they will be in a position to better service the exporting needs of regional manufacturers by incorporating various other factors into an ETC. This is probably one of the better examples of how an ETC can develop to directly involve small- and medium-sized firms. The principal shortcoming of such an ETC is its relative inability to establish substantial overseas networks. By including an export management company within its structure, the ETC can eliminate much of the problem. It will have difficulty, however, in attaining the foreign market coverage that a larger ETC will possess.

In addition to multinationals and regional governmental bodies forming ETCs, the U.S. banking community has expressed interest in this area. The ETC legislation opens many doors for banking institutions, allowing them to take advantage of the international services they currently provide and to package these services into an ETC that will perform a multitude of export functions. Since many banks already have extensive international networks, they can use their foreign contacts to relay market developments back to their home office, where product coordination enables them to supply various world markets. If the bank ETC has access to an array of marketable products in the U.S., it can use its information services, marketing services, and financial trade services to export U.S. goods and services overseas. The Bank of America, for example, is currently forming this kind of ETC. Bank ETCS realize the export potential of U.S. manufacturers and hope to coordinate their own international networks to facilitate the exporting needs of those producers who presently are not in the position to export.

Another well-publicized bank ETC is the one currently forming under the direction of Security Pacific Corporation. Its immediate goal is to form an ETC under its direct control, rather than to buy an export management company, which many major banks are currently proposing. This arrangement offers a clear advantage. Security Pacific can hire its own personnel and begin fresh—without obligations as to what goods will be dealt with or in what markets it will operate. On the other hand, such a start-up requires the development of a trading infrastructure, an expensive and time consuming process.

Although the ETC legislation has spurred interest in the area of export trading companies for years, many U.S. firms have been providing the same export services as an ETC. A trading house such as Boles and Company, Inc., for example, was designed according to the concept used by many of the larger foreign trading companies. By becoming totally market driven, rather than showing any product preference, these trading houses can deal in almost any product and enter any foreign market that shows potential. They are not limited by cumbersome infrastructures, but rely on market information and worldwide manufacturer contacts to supply what they see as high-potential markets abroad. These companies essentially act as "one-stop" exporting firms, taking title to the goods they sell and often playing the role of a broker, should the situation require such a service. Consider, for example, how Boles and Company was drawn into the European wine market. Boles realized the potential certain California wines had in the European market, and the company initiated an export effort after repackaging and labelling the wine.

The growing trend toward countertrade, including counterpurchase and import compensation arrangements, means that many U.S. ETCs can no longer avoid these transactions. The current overvalued position of the U.S. dollar in world foreign exchange markets hinders the U.S. exporters' ability to compete. For this reason, and others, many larger trading companies are becoming involved in the area of countertrade and barter. Most ETCs are becoming more aware of the concept of countertrade, and in some instances, they are developing in-house countertrade services to market to other ETCs and multinational firms.

From these examples, we can see that the Export Trading Company Act is having the effect on U.S. exporting that Congress intended. It will take time, however, before actual trade figures can support the current activity within the ETC industry. We expect to see the export trading company industry expand as new foreign markets open, and the industry as a whole becomes more specialized and diversified in order to compete with the older, established, foreign trading companies.

2

Eleanor Roberts Lewis

Export Trade Certificates of Review*

The Export Trading Company Act of 1982 provides for a certificate of review program that enables businesses engaged in export trade to determine in advance whether their proposed export conduct will have specific protection from liability under federal and state antitrust laws. Under the certification procedure described in the statute, the Commerce Department must determine, with the concurrence of the Justice Department, whether an applicant's proposed conduct meets the definitions and standards for eligibility set out in Title III of the Export Trading Company Act. See Pub. L. No. 97-290, 96 Stat. 1233-1247 (1982) (to be codified at 15 U.S.C. 4011-4021). The mechanics of the certification procedure are established in interim regulations published by the Department of Commerce. 48 F.R. 10595 (March 11, 1983) (to be codified at 15 C.F.R. Part 325). In addition, the Department of Commerce has published *Guidelines for the Issuance of Export Trade Certificates of Review* which analyzes the eligibility definitions and

*The views expressed in this chapter are those of the author and do not necessarily reflect those of the Department of Commerce. Ms. Lewis would like to thank Janice Payt for her assistance in preparing the chapter.

standards. 48 F.R. 15937 (April 13, 1983). The Department of Justice concurred in both the regulations and guidelines.

PERSONS ELIGIBLE FOR CERTIFICATION

The Act provides that any "person" may apply for a certificate of review. According to Title III, a "person" can be any of the following: (1) an individual who is a United States resident; (2) a partnership that is created under and exists pursuant to state or federal laws; (3) a state or local government entity; (4) a corporation (profit or nonprofit) that is created under and exists pursuant to state or federal laws, or (5) any association or combination, by contract or other arrangement, between or among such persons. ETC Regulations, § 311(5).

The Title III definition of "person" is not limited solely to export trading companies. It also includes, for example, those companies for which export trade comprises only a small portion of business operations. Although the Title III definition of "person" does not allow foreign firms to apply for a certificate directly, U.S. subsidiaries of foreign firms are eligible to apply, and foreign companies are also eligible to receive the protection of a certificate as members of an applicant U.S. trading entity. ETC *Guidelines* at II.

CONDUCT ELIGIBLE FOR CERTIFICATION

Conduct that constitutes export trade, export trade activities, or methods of operation, as those terms are defined in Section 311 of the ETC Act, is eligible for certification. The ETC *Guidelines* indicate that the government will ordinarily determine, as a threshold matter, whether the proposed conduct falls within these definitions before considering whether the conduct meets the substantive eligibility standards of Section 303(a) of the Act. ETC *Guidelines* at IV.

Export Trade

Title III defines "export trade" as "trade or commerce in goods,

ABOUT THE AUTHOR

Eleanor Roberts Lewis is assistant general counsel for export trading companies at the United States Department of Commerce. In that position, she is the senior staff attorney responsible for the Commerce Department's implementation of the Export Trading Company Act of 1982. Ms. Lewis came into the job after three years as assistant general counsel for finance at the U.S. Department of Housing and Urban Development. Before that, she was associated with the Washington, D.C., law firm of Brownstein, Zeidman, and Schomer. Ms. Lewis is the author or editor of several articles and books on legal topics. She has a B.A. from Wellesley College, an M.A. from Harvard University, and a J.D. from Georgetown University.

wares, merchandise, or services exported, or in the course of being exported, from the United States or any territory thereof or to any foreign nation." ETC Regulations § 311(1).

While this definition is similar to that contained in the Webb-Pomerene Act (15 U.S.C. 61-65), it differs in its inclusion of the export of services, which are not protected by the Webb Act. And unlike the Bank Export Services Act found in Title II of the ETC Act, Title III does not require that the exported goods or services be produced in the United States. In addition, patent, trademark, know-how, and technology licensing of persons located in other countries is "export trade" that is eligible for certification.

Export Trade Activities and Methods of Operations

The Act defines "export trade activities" as "activities or agreements in the course of export trade." ETC Regulations § 311(3). "Methods of operation" is defined as "any method by which a person conducts or proposes to conduct export trade." ETC Regulations § 311(4). Whether conduct is best characterized as "export trade activity" or as "methods of operation" is not important for eligibility purposes, provided the proposed conduct comes within the purview of one or the other.

Export trade activities may include services that are provided exclusively to facilitate the export of goods or services, such as product research and design, financing, communication and processing of foreign orders, and negotiating export contracts with foreign buyers. Agreements in the course of export trade might include agreements among members on the allocation of export quotas; agreements to pool products for export shipment; agreements setting prices, terms, and conditions of sale in foreign markets; and distributorship agreements with foreign distributors. Methods of operation eligible for certification might include such mechanisms as using exclusive or nonexclusive foreign distributors, selling on consignment, and using a resale price maintenance program for an applicant's foreign sales.

While, as a general matter, overseas investment activities are not eligible for certification, they may be eligible where the investment is essential to the export of a good or service. For example, investment in warehouse facilities overseas to store exported products until they are transferred to the foreign purchaser would ordinarily be eligible. Similarly, patent, trademark, know-how, and technology licensing of persons located in other countries is "export trade" that is eligible for certification.

CERTIFICATION STANDARDS

Eligibility for certification is based on four specific standards set forth in Title III. The ETC *Guidelines* clarify that these certification standards are intended to encompass substantive American federal antitrust law as modified by the Webb-Pomerene Act. ETC *Guidelines* at V. The government's analysis will not be concerned with the impact of the proposed export conduct on foreign markets, competitors, or consumers. However, where proposed conduct will have a substantial anticompetitive impact on trade or commerce in the U.S., or on the export opportunities of other U.S. exporters, a certificate will not be issued. In sum, the standards should fulfill the important purpose of encouraging exports while still protecting American consumers and other American exporters from anticompetitive restraints. Let's look at each of the standards in turn.

1. Substantial Lessening of Competition or Restraint of Trade

Under this standard, proposed export conduct must not substantially lessen competition or restrain trade within the U.S. or substantially restrain the export trade of any competitor. ETCA, § 303(a)(1). To determine whether the proposed conduct will comply with this standard, the analysis will generally look to the overall purpose and effect of the activities on competition and whether the impact is unreasonably restrictive of competitive conditions.

The analysis for determining whether conduct under this first standard should be certified will, in most instances, be under the "rule of reason." The *Guidelines* indicate that when making this determination, the agencies will balance the likely procompetitive and anticompetitive effects of the proposed action within each relevant market. If the net impact of the restraint will not substantially lessen competition, it will be certified. Alternatively, if, for example, the exchange of price, output, or other sensitive information in the course of export trade will result in a substantial lessening of competition in the domestic market, that method of operation or activity will not be certified. ETC *Guidelines* at V. A.

2. Unreasonable Price Effects

Proposed conduct will meet this standard if it will not have the foreseeable consequence of unreasonably enhancing, stabilizing, or depressing prices in the United States. ETCA, § 303(a)(2). The *Guidelines* clarify that an increase in domestic price will not be "unreasonable" if it is caused only by export sales that lessen domestic supply because of a legitimate response to foreign demand. Conversely, "unreasonable" (and therefore uncertifiable) price increases will usually result from anticompetitive behavior directed at the domestic market, such as intentional manipulation of domestic prices through the manipulation of domestic supplies. ETC *Guidelines* at V. B. This interpretation signifies that joint export operations that result in increased overseas trade ecause of export efficiencies should be certifiable, even though a natural consequence in the United States may be higher domestic prices.

3. Unfair Methods of Competition

The third standard requires that export conduct must not constitute unfair methods of competition against competitors engaged in the export of the same class of goods or services. ETCA § 303(a)(3). While its language is similar to that contained in Section 5 of the Federal Trade Commission Act (15 U.S.C. 45), this standard is narrower than the Federal Trade Commission Act. Moreover, the policies and purposes underlying Title III are different from the Federal Trade Commission Act. In light of these differences, the *Guidelines* note that the judicial decisions interpreting Section 5 of the Federal Trade Commission Act, while illustrative, have only limited precedential significance. ETC *Guidelines* at V. C.

An example of conduct that might not meet this third standard is the deliberate and unreasonable restriction of domestic export competitors from their source of supply. On the other hand, the fact that export sales by the applicant or its members would displace sales of other U.S. exporters would not be grounds in itself for denying certification. ETC *Guidelines* at V. C.

4. Resales in the United States

Under this standard, proposed export conduct must not result in the sale for consumption or resale within the U.S. of the exported product or service. ETCA, § 303(a)(4). The purpose of the standard is to ensure that the anticompetitive effects, if any, of proposed export conduct do not have a domestic impact through the export and sub-sequent re-import of goods and services back into the United States.

In analyzing export conduct under this standard, the Departments of Commerce and Justice will look at whether the reentry of the goods for consumption or resale within the United States was "reasonably expected" at the time the application was submitted, and if so, whether the sale or consumption within the U.S. may have a significant domestic impact. The exportation of products or services that are incorporated into finished products overseas, or that are in any significant manner transformed in their character and then exported back into the United States, would not ordinarily be denied certification under this standard.

Thus, the standard should not generally apply to the reentry of goods that are manufactured overseas under a licensing agreement or that are assembled overseas incorporating U.S. components. ETC *Guidelines* at V. D.

PROTECTION CONFERRED BY CERTIFICATION

A certificate of review protects its holder and the members identified in it from civil and criminal liability under Federal and State antitrust laws for conduct specified in the certificate and carried out during its effective period in compliance with its terms and conditions. There are two narrow exceptions to the antitrust immunity provided by a certificate of review. First, the Department of Justice may bring an action against a certificate holder to enjoin conduct that threatens clear and irreparable harm to the national interest. ETCA, § 306(b)(5). It is probable that this narrow exception to a certificate holder's immunity will only be relevant in cases of military or other national emergency. Second, any person who has been injured by the certified conduct may bring a civil action for injunctive relief and actual damages for conduct that does not comply with the four substantive eligibility standards. ETCA, § 306(b)(1). Such a cause of action could arise if the certificate had been incorrectly issued by the government through misapplication of the four eligibility standards or if certified conduct no longer met the standards because of changed circumstances. ETC *Guidelines* at II.

There are, moreover, significant limitations on private suits commenced against a certificate holder. These will be discussed, in detail, in the next chapter.

The Departments of Commerce and Justice have expressed the opinion that the Act's protection extends to members, officers, directors, employees and agents of the certificate holder who carry out the activities specified in the certificate. ETC Regulations, Supplementary Information, 48 F.R. 10596. In addition, agreements with non-members, such as domestic suppliers and foreign competitors, can be certified. However, the certificate provides no protection for persons not identified in the certificate. Also, conduct that falls outside the scope of the certificate or violates its terms is *ultra vires* and would remain fully subject to criminal sanctions, as well as both private and governmental civil enforcement suits under U.S. antitrust laws. ETC *Guidelines* at II. The certificate also provides no protection if it was obtained by fraud because it is void from the beginning. ETCA, § 303 (f). Finally, exporters should be aware that other nations may have antitrust or competition laws with which they must comply. The certificate does not confer immunity from foreign competition laws.

THE APPLICATION PROCESS

An applicant must submit an application for a certificate of review to the Department of Commerce. Basically, an applicant will need to describe the nature and volume of its domestic and proposed export activities. ETC Regulations, § 325.3(b). The department must determine whether the application is properly prepared and can be deemed submitted under the Act within five days from the date the department receives submission. ETC Regulations, § 325.3(d). The department must then send a summary of the application to the Federal Register for publication 10 days after the application is deemed submitted. ETC Regulations, § 325.5(a). The Commerce Department, with the concurrence of the Justice Department, will make a decision whether to grant the certificate within 90 days of the date the application is deemed submitted. ETC Regulations, § 325.4. If circumstances indicate that the applicant has a special need for a quick decision on its application, an applicant may request expedited review. Both the Commerce and Justice Departments must agree with the applicant that expedited review is appropriate. If the request for expedited procedure is granted, the agencies will issue or deny a certificate within 45 days after an application is deemed submitted. ETC Regulations, § 325.7. Both the 90-day and 45-day deadlines may be tolled with the consent of the applicant due to the need for supplemental information or for further analysis. The regulations require that a summary of any issuance or denial of a certificate be published in the Federal Register. ETC Regulations, § 325.5(c). The interim regulations also establish procedures for amending, modifying, or revoking a certificate, and describe the record for a court reviewing the government's determinations. ETC Regulations §§ 325.6, 325.9, 325.10.

Confidential business and financial information submitted in an application is protected from public disclosure by the Act. ETCA, § 309. Generally, the Act prohibits the agencies from disclosing information if it is privileged or confidential, and if disclosing the information would cause harm to the person submitting it. ETC Regulations, § 325.14(b)(1). The regulations permit a person submitting information to designate the documents or information which it considers confidential in order to help the agencies determine whether information may be protected. ETC Regulations, § 325.14(b)(2). The government may, however, disclose confidential information under limited circumstances listed in the statute. ETCA, § 309(b)(2). If these circumstances arise, the government not only must attempt to notify the party who submitted the information of any request for disclosure, but may seek or support an appropriate protective order on behalf of the party who submitted the information. ETC Regulations, § 325.14(c). Finally, in implementing the certification program, the Departments of Commerce and Justice will take administrative measures, in addition to the statutory exemptions, to protect confidential commercial or financial information. For example, while an entire certificate may be available for public inspection in a Department of Commerce reading room, a certificate could generally be drafted so that it will not contain sensitive or confidential information.

CONCLUSION

Whether the certificate of review program will broaden the scope of export activity depends on the energies and ingenuity of exporters and on how the Departments of Commerce and Justice interpret their mandates. In addition, the potential applicant must weigh the protection offered by the certificate against the cost of preparing the application and the possible exposure of confidential business plans to the government and others. The Commerce Department guidelines and regulations emphasize the flexible approach the agencies intend to utilize in implementing the antitrust certification procedure. This approach, in combination with input from the private sector, should ensure that the program reflects business realities and provides a valuable process by which businesses can expand export operations.

3

Stanley J. Marcuss

Antitrust Protection for Export Trade

The Export Trading Company Act of 1982 is an important tool for improving America's ability to compete abroad. The Act seeks to increase United States exports of goods and services, in part by encouraging joint export activities that will enable United States exporters to compete more efficiently and effectively in foreign markets. To accomplish this objective, the Act removes some uncertainty as to liability under United States antitrust laws. In the past, this uncertainty deterred cooperation among United States exporters.

The antitrust provisions of the ETC Act are set forth in Titles III and IV. Title III establishes a certification process that enables businesses engaged in export trade to determine in advance whether their proposed export conduct will be partially insulated from liability under federal and state antitrust laws. Title IV, the Foreign Trade Antitrust Improvements Act of 1982, clarifies the applicability of United States antitrust jurisdiction to international business transactions.

Titles III and IV operate independently of each other. Thus, exporters have the choice of relying solely on Title IV or seeking a certificate of review under Title III. If the antitrust laws under Title IV do

ABOUT THE AUTHOR

Stanley J. Marcuss is a partner in the Washington, D.C., office of Milbank, Tweed, Hadley & McCloy. Prior to joining Milbank, he was the senior deputy assistant secretary of commerce. His duties included the administration of U.S. antidumping, export control, antiboycott, and foreign trade zone laws.

Among his other publications are works on the extraterritoriality of U.S. trade laws, U.S. antiboycott laws, the Export-Import Bank, and U.S. antidumping, countervailing duty, and unfair trade practices laws.

Mr. Marcuss is a summa cum laude graduate of Trinity College (Conn.), a graduate of Cambridge University, England, where he received B.A. and M.A. degrees in economics and law, and the Harvard Law School, where he received a J.D. in 1968.

not apply to the export activity at issue, there is no need to resort to the certification procedure.

TITLE IV — JURISDICTION OF U.S. ANTITRUST LAWS.

Title IV amends two of the major United States antitrust laws, the Sherman Act and the Federal Trade Commission Act. (As noted below, Title IV does not amend the Clayton Act.) Generally, the Sherman Act prohibits contracts, combinations, or conspiracies in restraint of trade, as well as monopolization or attempts to monopolize. Title IV adds a new Section 7 to the Sherman Act that provides that the Act does not apply to export trade unless there is a "direct, substantial, and reasonably foreseeable effect" on the domestic or import commerce of the United States or on the export opportunities of a domestic person. Title IV amends the Federal Trade Commission Act to provide the same exemption from that statute's prohibition against unfair methods of competition for export trade activities that do not have a direct, substantial, and reasonably foreseeable effect on U.S. domestic commerce.

What Does "Direct, Substantial, and Reasonably Foreseeable" Mean?

The new standard clarifies the test for determining the applicability of United States antitrust jurisdiction to international transactions. Under the "effects test" originally formulated by the courts, United States antitrust laws encompassed acts outside the United States if the acts affected U.S. commerce and were intended to do so. Later interpretations of this test differed concerning the nature and magnitude of the effect necessary for the antitrust laws to apply.

For example, the Justice Department's 1977 Antitrust Guide to International Operations required a direct, substantial, and foreseeable effect on U.S. commerce. In contrast, some courts required that there be only a "direct" effect. One court stated that the effect probably did not have to be substantial and direct so long as it was not *de minimus.* Other courts adopted a "balancing approach." In other words, a court was required to weigh numerous factors, ranging from the nationality of the parties to the foreseeability of the effects of the conduct on U.S. commerce, in order to determine whether the jurisdiction of the antitrust laws extended to a particular international transaction. It remains to be seen exactly how the courts will apply the new Title IV standard, but it seems likely that such balancing approaches will be rejected in determining international jurisdiction.

A few common situations illustrate the impact of the new Section 7 of the Sherman Act. American competitors who combine solely to export, for example, are protected from Sherman Act liability unless their export conduct has a direct, substantial, and foreseeable effect on competition within the United States, among United States firms, or on the export trade of a U.S.-based person. If the requisite effect of such person's export commerce exists, the Sherman Act applies only to the extent of injury to export trade in the United States.

Section 7 also provides some protection for tie-in arrangements in which the sale of one product (the "tying" product) is dependent upon the buyer's purchase of a second product (the "tied" product). Such arrangements are protected from Sherman Act liability when the only injured parties are foreign customers and excluded foreign competitors. But if the tie-in excludes a U.S. competitor engaged in export trade and

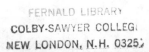

such effect were direct, substantial, and reasonably foreseeable, liability can exist under the Sherman Act.

Exclusive dealing arrangements between American firms and foreign distributors receive similar protection. Under an exclusive dealing arrangement, an American firm may require a foreign distributor not to deal in the goods of the American firm's competitors. The Sherman Act, as amended, protects such arrangements to the extent that the excluded competitors and injured consumers are foreigners.

Title IV does *not* exempt joint ventures engaged in export trade from liability under Section 7 of the Clayton Act, which prohibits mergers that may substantially lessen competition or tend to create a monopoly. Title IV, as originally introduced in Congress, would have amended Section 7 of the Clayton Act to exempt such joint export ventures, but the provision was eliminated as part of a last minute compromise. Thus, exporters engaged in joint ventures who are concerned about potential Clayton Act liability cannot rely solely on Title IV for antitrust protection. Such exporters may seek protection from such liability by applying for an export certificate of review under Title III of the ETC Act.

TITLE III — CERTIFICATES OF REVIEW

Title III of the ETC Act establishes an antitrust preclearance mechanism for U.S. exporters that entitles the holder of a certificate of review to a limited antitrust exemption, as discussed in the prior chapter. One should note, however, that a certificate holder remains potentially liable to a private party who is injured by (1) export activities covered by a certificate if such activities do not comply with the four standards set forth in Title III, and (2) activities that are not covered by or do not conform to the certificate. If a plaintiff can prove the latter type of activities, the Title III immunity would be irrelevant, and the plaintiff could seek treble damages under the Sherman Act.

If the challenged activities are covered by a certificate, there are three significant limitations on a private right of action against the holder of such certificate. First, remedies are limited to injunctions and recovery of actual (rather than treble) damages. Second, the private plaintiff bears the burden of overcoming a statutory presumption that conduct that is specified in and complies with a certificate does indeed conform to the antitrust standards of the ETC Act, and, therefore, is exempt from antitrust liability. If the private plaintiff fails to overcome such presumption, he is liable for the defendant's litigation costs, including reasonable attorney's fees. Presumably, this liability for attorneys' fees, plus the need to overcome the legal presumption, should be significant deterrents, especially since a plaintiff could at best recover only actual damages. Third, suit must be brought within two years of discovery of the violation of the Title III certification standards and not later than four years after the violation has occurred.

A certificate does not protect its holders from antitrust liability in several other circumstances. A certificate provides no protection if the holder obtained it by fraud. Also, the certificate does not confer immunity from foreign antitrust laws, and thus certificate holders remain subject to suit by competitors or foreign governments under foreign competition laws.

Title III sets forth the procedural requirements for certification. It specifies the information that must be in the application for a certificate and establishes various time limits for issuance or denial of a certificate, for appeal of a denial of a certificate, and for publication in the Federal Register of notices of applications and appeals. In addition, Title III establishes expedited review provisions if the applicant indicates a special need for prompt disposition, as well as procedures for amendment and revocation of a certificate.

Title III protects confidential information submitted to the government during the certification process. The mandatory disclosure requirements of the Freedom of Information Act do not apply to information submitted by an applicant for a certificate of review. Furthermore, federal employees are prohibited from disclosing confidential or privileged commercial or financial information if disclosure would harm the applicant. There are, however, certain circumstances in which disclosure of such information is permissible, such as when the information is sought by Congress or for judicial or administrative proceedings, or when disclosure is required by statute. Title III also gives the secretary of commerce broad discretion to disclose confidential information if necessary to determine whether to issue a certificate.

Publication in the Federal Register of the general outline of an application for a certificate is one of several potential disadvantages of using the certification procedure under Title III. Some critics contend that such disclosure could lead to greater scrutiny of an application, thereby increasing the likelihood of litigation by the applicant's competitors. In any event, whatever is disclosed in the Federal Register notice would presumably be no more than what such competitors would know in the absence of such publication. Another disadvantage is the expense of applying for a certificate of review. Furthermore, it is unlikely that the government will grant a certificate for export conduct that falls within the gray area of antitrust liability. Thus, those exporters that are uncertain about their antitrust liability will be less likely to benefit from the certification procedure. Exporters who seek but do not obtain a certificate would be in an uncomfortable situation if they still desired to engage in the proposed conduct: They may be effectively prevented from doing so because they will have alerted the government and competitors to conduct that might otherwise have gone unnoticed.

On the other hand, there are several significant advantages under Title III. The certification process enables one to reduce the uncertainty and risks of antitrust liability by knowing the government's position before engaging in certain export conduct. Moreover, certification under Title III provides immunity under all antitrust laws, and thus offers some protection for joint ventures.

CONCLUSION

Although the Export Trading Company Act of 1982 provides U.S. exporters with some protection from the threat of antitrust liability, it is not a panacea. Before engaging in joint export trade activities, a company must, therefore, carefully consider any potential antitrust problems relating to such activities. A company can simply rely on Title IV or affirmatively seek to take advantage of the certification procedure under Title III. While Title IV offers less protection from antitrust liability, it nonetheless avoids some of the pitfalls of Title III. Thus, before applying for a certificate, exporters should carefully weigh the potential risks and benefits available under the Title III certification program and determine whether the Title IV immunity would be sufficient for the proposed export activities.

4

Leo G. B. Welt

Countertrade as a Tool for ETCs

As world competition for export markets becomes increasingly intense, more and more export-related companies are seeking ways to enhance their international trade advantages. One tool, in particular, answers to demands that are peculiar to today's international marketplace. The tool is countertrade—a form of financing that has evolved in response to situations in which would-be recipients of exports offer payment in kind rather than cash for goods.

Trade with Chinese, East European, Soviet, and Third World markets is often contingent on this form of payment. If a company does not have the ability to negotiate such arrangements, it runs the risk of losing the sale to more adroit competitors, primarily European and Japanese firms, who already have both the experience and the inclination to undertake countertrade ventures.

Only by developing the capacity to trade competitively—by offering similar kinds of finance arrangements—will U.S. ETCs be able to meet the demands of current market situations. Thus, as they set out to establish themselves, ETCs will have to concentrate one part of their efforts on developing some form of countertrade capability.

Countertrade, predictably, is more complex than straight cash-for goods transactions. The process involves negotiating and signing additional contracts. This, and the task of disposing of countertraded goods, all add to the complications of the firm's business.

However, indications of the rising demand for countertrade are reflected in U.S. Department of Commerce estimates made in 1976 that 28 percent of all East-West trade was, in fact, some form of countertrade. About half the contracts now signed in connection with East-West trade are countertrade.

Specific measures recently enacted by some foreign governments will contribute to this growing countertrade activity. They include:

- *Minimum export sales levels set by governments in some developing and socialist countries to spur the marketing of their products, ensure employment for their citizens, and to obtain foreign exchange.* Brazil, for example, requires any foreign company building a factory under pioneer status to export a given percentage of the plant's production.
- *Import restrictions imposed by governments to cut foreign currency drains.* Countertrade is a means of working within such import restrictions. Brazil, for example, agreed to purchase foreign mining shovels with Brazilian iron ore.
- *Countertrade demands made by socialist and Third World countries.* These countries, with few marketing channels, are making countertrade demands to create markets for their goods.

DISPOSING OF GOODS

The ability of an ETC to efficiently dispose of goods received in countertrade will often determine the profitability of the deal. The trading company does just that—its job is to find a market for the goods and/or materials it acquires.

Trading Houses or Trading Companies

For the ETC that rarely deals in countertrade and has little desire to establish its own countertrade unit—as is often the case with many of the smaller regional and product-specific ETCs—it is usually preferable to contract the services of a trading house. The first step is to select a trading house whose specializations in terms of product and geographical area of expertise suit the company's needs.

Brokers. Some trading houses work as middlemen, or brokers, trying to bring together sellers and buyers of particular items—without taking title to the goods. Their primary activity is to keep abreast of the needs of companies in a particular industry and to come up with supplies of inputs for production for the customers that engage their service.

Principals. Other trading houses play a more active role, that of principals, who buy and resell the items they acquire. If the trading company does not have a customer at the time of the acquiring, it will stockpile the goods for a future sale.

Consultants. Trading companies also act as consultants. An ETC might hire a trading house to provide information and give advice as to what kinds of items it should obtain to fulfill a countertrade obligation. Trading houses that specialize in one particular country or small group of countries will usually have at their fingertips a large reservoir of information and expertise to help steer ETCs away from goods that are undesirable because they are difficult to resell.

Disadvantages

The profit margins of trading houses are generally said to be one-half to 4 percent for low-risk items and 15 to 20 percent for higher risk categories. In addition to this disadvantage—having either to pay a commission, or perhaps to sell the countertraded item at a discount—the company that relies on a trading house also fails to gain knowledge of the market, which it would otherwise do if it negotiated its own sales. Thus, it will continue to be dependent on the services of a trading house.

If using a trading house proves unsatisfactory, the ETC has the option of establishing its own countertrade unit. Many ETCs are doing so.

IN-HOUSE TRADING UNITS

Companies that deal extensively in countertrade often set up in-house countertrade units. They have been motivated to do so because in the past they have been forced to choose between two undesirable alternatives: using a trading company or abstaining from deals involving countertrade. The first alternative results in a loss of profit, the second in a loss of potential sales.

In addition to helping an ETC fulfill countertrade obligations, the countertrade unit often takes on outside clients. The rationale is obvious: Since the ETC countertrade unit has acquired expertise and experience, it makes business sense to market that knowledge.

TYPES OF COUNTERTRADE

The forms of countertrade vary but can be roughly divided into the following categories.

Barter

This form of countertrade is the easiest to understand: it involves goods for goods, usually with only one contract and no cash changing hands. An example of how vast the scope of a barter deal can be is the 20-year agreement whereby Occidental Petroleum Corporation has contracted to ship one million tons of phosphate rock annually to Poland in exchange for an annual shipment of half a million tons of Polish molten sulfur.

Barter can involve more than two parties, as in the deal by which Israel sent potash to Poland, which sent an equal-value shipment of sugar to Brazil, which closed the transaction by sending an equal-value shipment of coffee to Israel. No money changed hands.

Counterpurchase

In this form of countertrade a company sells equipment or products to another country or party for cash *plus* products. A contract clause stipulates that the vendor counterpurchase a given percentage of the contract value in the form of products from the buyer's country. For example, Fried. Krupp Huttenwerke AG of West Germany won a $9 million order for big capacity hydraulic cranes from the Soviet company MACHINOIMPORT by agreeing to buy back 15 percent of the contract value in Soviet machine tools and equipment. Krupp was prepared for the countertrade demand and was able either to use the machines and equipment in its West German plants or resell them. Krupp's competitors in the deal, which included two U.S. companies, Grove Manufacturing Co. and Harnischfeger Corporation, and a British firm, Coles Crane, were not prepared to accept the countertrade requirements. They would have been forced to sell the counterpurchased goods on the open market at a discount of up to 40 percent, which made the deal unattractive.

Counterpurchase can be a useful tool for companies seeking to enter new markets and gain an edge over competitors. An example is McDonnell Douglas Corporation's success in Yugoslavia. To close a major Yugoslav purchase of DC-9 passenger jets, McDonnell Douglas agreed to buy canned hams, tools, and other products from that country. McDonnell Douglas' counterpurchase, or "offset program" as company officials call it, eventually evolved into a large, ongoing business arrangement. As part of its countertrade in Yugoslavia, McDonnell Douglas now actively encourages its employees and their families to fly on JAT Yugoslav airlines and to vacation on that Adriatic country's seashore.

Compensation

This form of countertrade is usually part of an industrial cooperating agreement or a joint venture without equity. In a compensation arrangement, a company sells machinery, equipment, technology, or a turn-key plant and receives the resultant products as full or partial payment. International Harvester Corp., for example, sold the technology for making crawler tractors to the Polish foreign trade organization Bumar. As payment, International Harvester agreed to *buy back* at a discount a percentage of the components made at the Polish plant for use at its own plants in Western Europe. Levi-Strauss & Company made a similar agreement with Hungary. It sold a turn-key plant and the design of its famous blue jeans to Hungary in return for a portion of the plant's production.

Swap

The "swap" concept is simple enough. Products from different locations are traded to save transportation costs. This is ideally suited for such commodities as sugar, chemicals, ore, and oil. The swap of Soviet oil bound for Cuba and Mexican oil heading for Europe illustrates the swap transaction. In a recent agreement, the Soviets supplied oil to Mexico's customers in Gelsenkirchen, West Germany, and in Eastern Europe, while Mexico supplied oil to Cuba. Thus, both countries save considerable transportation cost. In swap transactions, differences in the quality of the goods being substituted are worked out in the contract.

Clearing Agreements

Clearing agreements are bilateral arrangements between two countries to purchase designated amounts of each other's products over a specific period of time. The countries also agree to use a stipulated "clearing currency" in the transactions, such as the U.S. dollar, the French franc, or another freely convertible currency. Clearing agreements help countries maintain better trade balances and assure export markets for some of their goods. While clearing agreements may be new to Americans, they are common in the developing world and in countries with state-controlled economies.

Clearing agreements were common in Europe after World War II because of the short supply of cash and the low trade value of the currencies of many European nations. Although the number of clearing agreements has declined over the last two decades, they are still used frequently in some countries. A recent survey reported that the USSR has 30 such agreements, Mexico 19, and Brazil 17. Many clearing agreements have clauses that allow the "switch" of all or part of the bilateral trade balance to a third party. The "switch" is yet another form of countertrade.

Switch

This method of countertrade is useful when international currency flow is sluggish or uneven. One of the countries that is a party in a bilateral trade agreement will transfer its imbalance to a third party or nation. For example, a Western firm sought to sell a plastic-manufacturing plant to the USSR, which did not have the cash to pay for it. However, the Soviet Union had a clearing agreement with Austria, which was buying Russian natural gas. So instead of Austria paying the USSR for the gas, Austria paid the Western firm an amount corresponding to the price of the factory.

Evidence Accounts

These are agreements for a certain amount of purchase and selling between a company and local foreign trade organizations. The agreements are monitored by the bank of foreign trade located in that country, where the foreign party to the agreement maintains an account. In the evidence account agreement, the local company sells goods or services to one foreign trade organization, while simultaneously buying certain products from another foreign trade organization to balance the account. These transactions are set to occur over a specified period, commonly one year.

Blocked Currencies

When a company or individual is unable to repatriate holdings or funds from a country because of currency restrictions, several methods can be employed to use up the accumulated money locally and get products out of the country that can be sold for cash. Some companies buy local products with local currency, then export them. In addition, these funds are sometimes used to make movies within the country, using the local currency for that purpose. The movie can then be taken out of the country with no problem.

Development For Import (DFI)

Development for import agreements occur in situations where

industries attempt to secure a constant supply of raw materials from another country, with the aid of their own governments. The government of one nation will make low interest loans available to domestic companies in order to aid in the development of a particular supply of raw materials in another foreign market. The Japanese government, for example, made such low interest loans available to Japanese firms to aid in the development of iron ore resources in Australia.

PROS AND CONS OF COUNTERTRADE

The economic costs of countertrade are considered to be the major disadvantage of using this kind of trade finance. However, for companies now debating the pros and cons of starting up a countertrade operation, it is worthwhile to point out that although the costs of countertrade agreements can run high in some cases, the economic benefits almost invariably outweigh the costs.

Countertrade can indeed add to the complexities of an already complex business. The increased paperwork associated with two- and three contract deals, combined with the increased use of valuable executive time, can result in distortions of both prices and markets in international trade. These factors must be given careful consideration by any ETC before it undertakes to develop its own countertrade unit and actually negotiate such deals for itself.

But American business must not seek to avoid the complexities of countertrade. Rather, they must *adapt* to practices that have for years been utilized—and continue to be utilized—by foreign trading companies to tap otherwise inaccessible markets. If U.S. ETCs truly wish to compete internationally on a level with other foreign trading companies, they must accept the change in world markets and position themselves so that they can capitalize on them. Gaining the expertise and experience needed to employ countertrade methods of finance will give them this edge.

5

James S. Keller

ETCs: The Perspective of the Federal Reserve Board*

When export trading company legislation was pending before Congress, the Federal Reserve Board took a very restrictive approach toward the role that banking organizations should have with respect to these entities. The board expressed its concern, through testimony on the several bills that were considered, that if banking organizations were able to have controlling equity interests in companies engaged in a large range of commercial activities, there would be a substantial breakdown in the barriers between banking and commerce.

The board maintained that the longstanding policy of the separation of banking and commerce deserved continued support because it addressed two principal concerns: (1) the safety and soundness of banks might be impaired by close affiliation with potentially high-risk commercial operations, and (2) available credit might be allocated on a basis other than the borrower's creditworthiness. A bank might be

*The views expressed are those of the author and not necessarily those of the Board of Governors or members of its staff.

ETCs: New Methods for U.S. Exporting—45

ABOUT THE AUTHOR

For the past year, **James S. Keller** has been manager of the International Applications Section in the Federal Reserve Board's Division of Banking Supervision and Regulation. From 1977 to 1982, Mr. Keller was on the staff of the board's legal division, where he worked primarily on bank holding company and international matters. Before joining the board, he served as a law clerk to the Honorable Harold H. Greene, who was then Chief Judge of D.C. Superior Court.

Mr. Keller received his J.D. from George Washington University School of Law in 1975 and his B.A. from Harvard College in 1966.

enticed into giving preferential treatment to its affiliate's customers, for example, or into denying credit to its affiliate's competitors.

The board made a number of legislative proposals that would maintain a maximum separation of banking and commerce, while allowing banking organizations to acquire an equity interest in export trading companies. These proposals included: limiting the percentage of ownership a bank holding company could have in an export trading company; restricting ownership to bank holding companies rather than allowing banks and other depository institutions to own export trading companies directly; prohibiting joint venture ownership of export trading companies by banking and nonbanking organizations; prohibiting bank-affiliated export trading companies from taking title to goods except against firm orders; prohibiting an export trading company from using the name of an affiliated banking organization; and prohibiting a bank-affiliated export trading company from engaging in any manufacturing, including product modification.

In enacting the Bank Export Services Act (BESA), which is Title II of the Export Trading Company Act of 1982, Congress adopted only one of the board's recommendations: that equity interests in export trading companies could be held only through bank holding companies.[1]

[1]An export trading company may also be owned through a bankers' bank or an Edge Corporation that is owned by a bank holding company (but not by an Edge Corporation owned by a bank). The bank holding company form of ownership can be expected to be the form selected by most banking organizations.

Furthermore, the legislation reflected congressional wariness of the board's view of bank affiliation with export trading companies; rather than requiring prior board approval for the establishment or acquisition of an export trading company, the BESA contains a prior notification procedure that severely limits the basis on which the board may deny a bank holding company's notification to acquire an equity interest in an export trading company.

THE BOARD'S REGULATIONS

In response to the legislation, the board adopted very brief regulations, mainly to clarify a few areas of ambiguity in the statutory language. For the most part, these clarifications reflect an attempt to limit the potential for conflicts of interest that might grow out of bank affiliation with an export trading company. At the same time, they reflect recognition of the congressional intent that the board help promote the development of these entities.

In adopting its final regulations,[2] the board focused on a few issues of concern. One basic issue—widely discussed in the public's comments on the proposed regulations and at the board meeting at which the regulations were adopted—was the definition of an export trading company in which a bank holding company may invest. The board was concerned because the statutory language could be interpreted to permit a bank holding company to invest in any service company that principally provides its own services to non-U.S. residents. For example, the statute might be read to permit an insurance company that underwrites life or general insurance to qualify as an export trading company that could be owned by a bank holding company as long as the customers were non-U.S. residents. The board, however, read the legislative history of the BESA to support the interpretation adopted in its regulation—namely, that a bank holding company-owned export trading company should serve principally as an intermediary for producers and suppliers of goods and services in the foreign marketing and sale of their products by providing a range of export services.

[2]Promulgated on June 2, 1983 (48 Fed. Reg. 26,445 (1983)), as section 211.34 of the board's Regulation K. See Appendix A.

The board also attempted to clarify the statutory requirement that a bank holding company-controlled ETC should be "principally engaged in exporting." The board determined that a 50 percent test would be liberal yet consistent with the congressional purpose of promoting *exports*, not simply trade: At least half of the revenues of a bank holding company-controlled export trading company, as measured over a two-year period, must be derived from exporting, or facilitating the exportation of, goods. In this regard, trade between third countries (two countries other than the United States) and countertrade (an export from a third country undertaken as a *quid pro quo* for allowing U.S. goods to be imported into that country) are *not* to be included as exports for the purposes of meeting the 50 percent test. Again, the rationale for this determination was that the BESA was export legislation, not trade legislation. Furthermore, these types of transactions might result in providing substitutes for the export of U.S. goods.

Another controversial issue involved the collateral restrictions of Section 23A of the Federal Reserve Act (12 U.S.C. § 371c). Should these restrictions apply to transactions between a bank holding company-owned ETC and its affiliated bank? The question arose because of the provision in the BESA regarding the application of these collateral restrictions, and the subsequent amendment to Section 23A contained in the Garn-St. Germain Depository Institutions Act of 1982. While some argued that, on the basis of the statutory language and its legislative history, these collateral provisions should not apply, the board, nevertheless, applied the provisions to loans and extensions of credit by a bank to its affiliated export trading company. The board included in its regulations a waiver of the collateral requirements for two situations: (1) where the bank provides a letter of credit for the account of its affiliated export trading company or advances funds for the purchase of goods (for the resale of which the export trading company has a firm order); and (2) where the bank has a security interest in the goods, (or proceeds from the sale of the goods), equal to the value of the letter of credit or advance. Furthermore, the board indicated in adopting its regulations that it might grant additional waivers based on specific requests.

The board also addressed several procedural issues: whether to adopt a "general consent" procedure for export trading company investments, and what type of additional notices should be required by a bank holding company that seeks to expand its ETC's scope of activities. With respect to the former question, the board did not adopt expedited procedures for bank holding company investments in export trading companies, but stated its intention to reconsider adopting such procedures no later than June 2, 1984. With respect to additional notices, the board's regulations require that a bank holding company notify the board if an affiliated export trading company expands its activities beyond those described in the initial notice to include (1) taking title to goods, (2) product research and design, (3) product modification, or (4) activities not specifically spelled out in the BESA as export trade services. These activities, which are more commercial and less financial in nature, are the ones that cause the board particular concern.

In adopting its regulations, the board also noted that it was concerned with the leveraging ratios (assets to capital) of export trading companies, particularly where the company is engaged in taking title to goods and the investment in the export trading company is significant. The board stated that it would consider adopting industry-wide capital standards for bank-affiliated export trading companies. The board would consider adopting such standards on the basis of its further experience in processing notifications, but in no event later than June 2, 1984. The board also stated that it would review the capital adequacy of those bank holding companies seeking to make investments in export trading companies.

NOTIFICATIONS ACTED UPON TO DATE

In the year since the enactment of the BESA, the board has acted upon 11 notifications by bank holding companies to establish export trading companies (see the box on pp. 50-51). One can generally say, therefore, that there has not been an overwhelming rush by banking organizations to engage in this activity. Furthermore, the proposals have been conservative, especially with respect to the activities to be engaged in. It would appear, for example, that the banking organizations proposing to establish export trading companies are as concerned as the board

Bank Holding Company/ETC Notifications

Bank Holding Company	Date of Board Action
Security Pacific Corporation, San Francisco, CA	5/09/83
Citicorp, New York, NY	5/31/83
Walter E. Heller International Corporation, Chicago, IL	6/13/83
First Interstate Bancorp, Los Angeles, CA	6/15/83
Union Bancorp, Los Angeles, CA	7/25/83
First Kentucky National Corporation, Louisville, KY	7/25/83
Crocker National Corporation, San Francisco, CA	8/30/83

about the possibility of carrying an inventory of unsalable goods; accordingly, almost all the proposals to date that involve taking title to goods have stipulated that the bank-affiliated export trading company would take title to goods only against firm orders, even though the BESA has no such requirement.

The only other issue raised by the notifications to date relates to leveraging. The board has reiterated (in several of its letters transmitting the board's action on export trading company investments) its intent to issue industry-wide capital adequacy standards for bank holding company-controlled export trading companies. In the meantime, it has noted that, for at least one organization, a leveraging ratio for assets-to-capital of 10 to 1 would be acceptable.

The board recently acted upon a notification by three New Jersey

Ramapo Financial Corp, Wayne, NJ; Ultra Bancorporation, Bridgewater, NJ; and New Jersey National Corporation, Trenton, NJ	9/14/83
State Street Boston Corporation Boston, MA	9/19/83
International Bancshares Corporation, Laredo, TX	10/03/83
United Midwest Bancshares, Inc. Cincinnati, OH	10/26/83
U.S. Bancorp, Portland, OR	Pending
First Chicago Corporation, Chicago, IL	Pending
Ranier Bancorporation, Seattle, WA	Pending

bank holding companies to form a joint venture export trading company. In acting upon this notification, the board determined that the export trading company would be an affiliate of each bank holding company for the purposes of section 23A of the Federal Reserve Act. Under the proposal, each bank holding company is to hold less than 25 percent of the voting shares of the export trading company but more than 30 percent of its total equity.

The board is currently processing a notification by a bank holding company wishing to engage in joint venture ownership of an export trading company by sharing ownership with a nonbank organization (First Chicago Corporation/Sears World Trade). While the board had originally contended that such affiliations should not be permitted, the legislation specifically refers to the facilitation of joint venture export trading companies between bank holding companies and nonbank firms. The potential Sears-First Chicago Corporation joint venture is a case in point.

REPORTING AND EXAMINATION

The board has not adopted special reporting forms or developed specific instructions to its examiners with respect to export trading companies. Board staff recommended that within the first year of an export trading company's establishment, an on-site examination should be made of that subsidiary. Thereafter, its examination could be included as part of the overall inspection of the bank holding company, unless particular circumstances dictate otherwise.

It has also not yet been determined what reporting should be required of an export trading company, beyond its inclusion in the bank holding company's annual report to the board (Board Form F.R. Y-6). It is likely that the board would want to receive at least free-form financial statements (income statements and balance sheets, for example) on a more frequent basis (quarterly or semiannually). However, this determination has not yet been made.

CONCLUSION

While the board initially resisted the legislation enabling bank holding companies to invest in export trading companies, it has reacted to the legislation with brief regulations reflecting the spirit of the congressional intent—that the board help to promote (or at least not be an obstacle to the development of) bank-affiliated export trading companies. On the other hand, the banking organizations that fought so hard for the legislation appear to have taken a very cautious approach. Growth in this activity will probably be quite gradual. This should give the industry and the board the opportunity to ensure that business is conducted in a manner that, while promoting exportation of goods, will not impair the safety and soundness of the parent bank holding companies or their subsidiary banks.

6

Stephen R. Finch

The Role of Banks in ETCs

The Bank Export Services Act (BESA) of 1982 invites banks to become involved in commercial activity to an extent unparalleled since the passage of the Glass-Steagall Act. The driving force behind this invitation is the alarm felt by Congress and the administration over America's worsening balance of payments. A recent study by Chase Econometrics suggested that over 20,000 middle- and small-sized firms were not exporting, even though their products would be competitive on the world market. Historically, many of these firms either felt no need to export because of the size of the U.S. market or believed exporting to be too difficult and expensive to warrant their effort. Congress felt that the quickest way to create a conduit for these firms to international markets would be to utilize the capital, trade financing expertise, and worldwide networks of America's banking community through the format of Export Trading Companies (ETCs).

Given these policy reasons for Congress to grant this new privilege to bank holding companies, why should bankers cooperate? What incentives will induce banks to invest significant amounts of capital in a commercial area where they have little experience?

The obvious answer to these questions is the potential for greater

ABOUT THE AUTHOR

Stephen R. Finch is currently a second year student at the Harvard Business School where he is concentrating his studies in international business.

Previously, he was employed by the Department of Commerce, Office of Export Trading Company Affairs, where he counseled two major money center banks, two agribusiness firms, and a speciality steel manufacturer. In that position, he recommended optimal product/ market focus for developing an international trading business under the Export Trading Company Act of 1983. He also explained both new financing opportunities and liberalized antitrust provisions of the act.

Mr. Finch was also formerly with Shell Oil Company's Crude Oil Trading Department in Houston, Texas.

---

profit; however, it is not always clear how that increased profit potential will materialize. Certainly, the most obvious way for banks to profit from this opportunity is through the traditional exporting of domestically produced goods. However, Congress also gave bank-affiliated ETCs the right to export domestically produced services. Therein lie the most interesting possibilities for the banking community.

The term "export of services" has not yet acquired an exact defintion within the context of the BESA. A Federal Reserve Board (FRB) staff memo to the Board of Governors (dated May 2, 1983) took the concept of export of services to its logical conclusion by explaining that the statute raises the following issue:

> whether Congress intended through the BESA to authorize banking or- ganizations only to invest in a company that provides services to facilitate trade in goods and services produced by others, or whether Congress intended to grant the much broader authority to invest in any service company that principally provides its own services to nonresidents. That is, is any company that is a service company but which deals with foreign residents to be considered an "export trading company"?

The implications of such a definition for the international operations of

America's banks are astonishing. Essentially, banks would be immune to the limitations of the Glass-Steagall Act overseas. Through their ETCs, banks could own anything from an airline to a construction company. Already, some major New York banks have made tentative plans to start insurance companies.

Of course, the FRB has not been pleased with this threat of wholesale abandonment of the separation of commerce and banking overseas. Even more threatening to the FRB is the greater leverage banks would have with Congress in negotiating a revision of the Glass-Steagall Act if they had been investing de facto in commercial ventures overseas with no harm to depositors.

The FRB's reaction to this threat has been to severely limit the size of a bank-affiliated ETC through its definition of eligible revenues. Section 203 of the ETC Act of 1982 defines an ETC as a company:

> exclusively engaged in activities related to international trade, and which is organized and operated principally for purposes of exporting goods or services produced in the United States or for purposes of facilitating the exportation of goods or services produced in the United States by unaffiliated persons by providing one or more export trade services.

The FRB has interpreted that definition in its regulations (12 CFR § 211.32 (a)) as follows:

> exclusively engaged in activities related to international trade, and by engaging in one or more export trade services, derives more than half its revenues from the export of, or facilitating the export of, goods or services produced in the United States by persons other than the export trading company or its subsidiaries.

The difference between these two definitions is the scope of activities that will be counted as eligible revenue to meet the 50 percent criterion. The statutory definition seems to recognize revenues generated from either exporting its own goods and services or providing export trade services to others as eligible revenues for a bank ETC. However, the FRB regulation recognizes only those revenues derived from export trade services, such as arranging overseas freight for a client, as eligible. Since the potential revenue of export trade services is small compared to the potential of other services such as insurance, the 50 percent criterion places an effective constraint on the size of a bank-affiliated ETC. Thus, the FRB limits a bank holding company's exposure to commercial risk.

Clearly, this exposure is a legitimate area of concern for the FRB; however, the legislative history is ambiguous regarding the intent of Congress. Instead of concentrating on a palatable definition for export of services, the FRB has chosen to severely restrict an ETC's ability to export American produced goods as well. This step seriously jeopardizes the goal of Congress for bank participation in exporting. That goal is to create well capitalized ETCs that would accept the risk and rewards of aggressively marketing the products of America's small- and medium-sized producers from the factory gate to overseas consumers.

DESIGN FACTORS FOR ETCs

Despite the confusion in the regulatory environment, several bank ETCs have already been approved by the FRB, and numerous other bank holding companies are planning to form ETCs. This strategic planning stage of an ETC is perhaps the most important for determining the future ability of the new subsidiary to compete effectively.

The first choice a bank holding company must make when forming an ETC is how it can best take advantage of its new subsidiary to increase the total profitability of the firm. Possible ways of increasing profitability through an ETC include:

- Directly through trading operations.
- Indirectly through financing opportunities generated by ETCs.
- Indirectly through the normal banking business of new customers attracted by the availability of ETC services.
- Countertrade opportunities.

Other benefits which an ETC might bring to a bank include:

- More fee income.
- Demonstration of its aggressive posture and its commitment to innovation.

- More efficient utilization of global communication network and foreign offices.

A number of inherent risks counterbalance these benefits:

- *Cash drain.* Trading margins may be too slim to cover the increased fixed costs of the new subsidiary.
- *Trading risks.* Leftover unsalable goods, currency fluctuations, theft or damage of goods, nonpayment of accounts, and political instability.
- *Personnel.* Conservative bankers might not be able to acquire the skills and instincts of a trader. Conversely, traders might not accept a large bank's rigid personnel management system.
- *Regulatory.* The FRB might take a less favorable attitude toward a banks's other operations if its ETC is too aggressive vis-à-vis Glass-Steagall.
- *International.* The ETC might hurt the bank's relationship with its host governments overseas, which may be eager to correct their own balance of payments problems.

Once bank management determines the best strategy for profiting from its ETC, it must create an organization that can implement that strategy. Choosing the particular structure best suited for a bank-affiliated ETC begins with an analysis of how the above risk/reward tradeoffs can best be exploited given its unique financial, information management, and human resources. Most bank-affiliated ETCs can be categorized into four general models. Also, even though the ETC industry seems to have great room for expansion, bank management should consider what form competition might take in the future and which type of organization would give it the strongest market position. The following is a description of those models and examples of each.

1. Wholly owned, staffed by existing bank personnel

Using this model, a bank holding company would simply create a totally new subsidiary. Typically, it would be capitalized at between $10 and $40 million. The staff should be predominantly transfers from the international and trade finance divisions of the bank holding company's bank.

Most of the benefits of this model are derived from the familiarity with the bank's operations and style that the ETC staff will automatically have because of their banking background. This familiarity, along with existing informal relationships between the new ETC and bank personnel, will facilitate better coordination of ETC and bank functions. Additional benefits of this type of organization would include: trade financing and foreign exchange expertise; sensitivity to FRB regulations; and creation of alternate avenues of advancement for the bank's staff.

The disadvantages of this model are derived from the absence of marketing skills and from the risk aversion common to many bankers. Also, the bureaucratic systems normal in a large banking organization might be too cumbersome to permit an aggressive ETC operation. Finally, this model requires that the bank have a surplus of competent international bankers.

Examples of this option include Citicorp, Bank of America, and Union Bancorp. Citicorp is using its worldwide information network to arrange third-country countertrade deals. However, it is not taking possession of the goods. Instead, it is acting as a broker for a fee. In addition to countertrade, it is using its ETC to market the goods of countries heavily indebted to it, such as Mexico and Brazil.

Although it has not yet applied to the FRB, Bank of America was a strong supporter of the BESA and has formed a new subsidiary—Bank America World Trade. Union Bancorp of California is using its ETC to service its middle market customers through the worldwide network of its parent bank—Standard Chartered Bank of Great Britain.

2. Wholly owned, staffed with nonbanker international businessmen

A major concern of both the government and the banks themselves is the ease with which banks will be able to adapt to the commercial environment. This model addresses that issue by bringing in commercial expertise from outside the bank. Options for acquiring that expertise include recruiting individual international marketing executives or buying an export management company intact. The strengths and weaknesses of ETCs following this model are almost exactly the reverse of the model using the bank's existing staff.

Security Pacific, the first bank to receive FRB approval, has hired

Robert Van der Leek to become President and CEO of Security Pacific Trading Corp. He has had 20 years of international experience with Ford and Black and Decker and intends to complete his staff with other businessmen, not bankers.

Security Pacific is committed to making its ETC a totally new business opportunity. It will not be limited to soliciting the bank's customers only, nor will it be required to use the bank's financing if better terms are available elsewhere. Security Pacific's ETC has been given the most operational freedom of any bank ETC, which fits with their drive to diversify out of traditional commercial banking.

3. Joint venture with other banks

Small- and medium-sized banks might choose this option to share the risks and costs of operating an ETC. BITCO of Trenton, N.J., is the first joint venture of this type. It consists of Ramapo Financial Corp., New Jersey National, and Ultra Bancorp. It will focus on servicing the needs of its member banks' small- and medium-sized customers in central New Jersey.

Another version of this model is for several major regional banks from different areas to cooperate in forming one large, full-service ETC that would operate in each of their regions.

4. Joint venture with a commercial enterprise

Although it has not yet received approval from the FRB, First Chicago's proposed joint venture with Sears World Trade is the best example of this strategy. In testimony given before the Dixon Hearing in Chicago on July 15, 1983, Barry Sullivan, CEO of First Chicago Corporation, explained the working relationship between First Chicago and Sears World Trade as follows:

> A specially trained marketing team from First Chicago will originate potential trade transactions from our customer and prospect base, with emphasis on the Midwest, where first Chicago is historically well positioned. This team will marshal the resources of First Chicago's hundreds of relationship managers who will focus on recognizing product opportunities for the joint venture. Execution of trades, taking of title, logistics management, insurance, cargo handling, movement, and distribution of goods will then be effected by Sears World Trade, which has substantial worldwide expertise in these areas.

One of the exciting aspects of the joint venture is the global information capability. Through Sears World Trade's extensive worldwide network of experts in merchandising, the subsidiary will be able to gather, evaluate, and coordinate information about market needs worldwide.

In a sense, we are building on the example of highly successful nations such as Japan that have been able to expertly coordinate trade information and execution. We hope that we can improve on the model and significantly increase U.S. exports, including those from the Midwest.

We believe major impediments to trade have existed for U.S. manufacturers, especially for small- and medium-sized companies. These include the lack of access to market information, inadequate economies of scale, lack of experience in export management, and the lack of financing alternatives for foreign buyers. The inability to evaluate commercial and political risk has also been a limiting factor.

In this export trading company, First Chicago will function as the marketing force, bringing potential exporters to the joint venture for assistance. First Chicago will also have an opportunity to provide the necessary export/import financing, letters of credit, and other documentary and financial services as required.

First Chicago also expects to engage in countertrade activities through our joint venture with Sears World Trade. We have noted the increasing importance of this practice in world trade. Some estimates indicate that 20 percent of world trade is facilitated by means of countertrade.

Due to economic hardship and limited international currency reserves, some LDCs require that foreign exporters and contractors receive products in lieu of cash. Since many companies are unable to utilize the products offered in trade, we believe there is an opportunity to identify buyers or users of the LDCs' products and to participate in these trade flows as well.

While we may pursue these opportunities independently of the joint venture, some may be sufficiently large or complex as to require close cooperation with Sears World Trade.

Although his remarks are specific to First Chicago's arrangement with Sears World Trade, Mr. Sullivan has described the essential elements needed for any full service ETC.

- Recognizing exportable products.

- Understanding foreign markets.
- Arranging the actual transactions.
- Providing appropriate financing.
- Communicating trade information quickly and accurately around the world.

Developing an organization that can provide this entire range of services quickly and effectively will take time. However, before the banks begin that process in earnest, they will require clarification of the regulatory environment of their ETCs. Therefore, Congress must insure that its intentions for the BESA are correctly understood, both within government and in the banking community. Then, ETCs will be able to begin to play their role in alleviating America's balance of payments problem.

7

A. E. Klauser

Trading Companies: Japanese Models, American Responses

The development of Japan's pre-and postwar economy rests, in part, on the effectiveness of that country's general trading companies—the *sogo shosha*. Accounting for 55 percent of Japan's international trade, these huge enterprises have been copied by Korea, Taiwan, and Brazil, among other countries. And, in its effort to forge legislation and a national policy that would stimulate U.S. exports, Congress frequently cited examples of how these companies have contributed to export-led growth.

This chapter explores the background and workings of the *sogo shosha* in order to raise some important and basic questions: Can (or should) American enterprises and banks attempt to emulate these models? If not, are there any lessons from the Japanese experience that can help us develop our own American brand of ETC?

WHAT ARE *SOGO SHOSHA*?

Loosely translated, the words mean "general trading companies." Yet, this translation may not be appropriate. As Professor Yoshi Tsurumi observes, "In the West there are no equivalent counterparts of the *sogo shosha*[1]." Furthermore, these *sogo shosha* are changing constantly in order to adapt and operate successfully in the world's dynamic economic and political environment.

Currently, there are more than 11,000 trading companies in Japan, but the term *sogo shosha* is applied only to the nine largest. Most of the others, called *senmon shosha*, are small- or medium-sized firms, specializing in one or a few products or lines. The "Big Nine" are highly diversified and not only handle domestic trade between users and suppliers, but also engage extensively in all forms of international trade and commerce. Unlike the *senmon shosha*, they deal in virtually any type of product or commodity, and they often handle as many as 20,000 different items.

More specifically, these *sogo shosha* are large, broad-based, international trade intermediaries as well as creators of trade flows, and they offer a complete, integrated range of trading services. Their *raison d'etre* is to expedite and expand trade as well as develop future trade opportunities.

They are unique. Unlike manufacturers, who are user-maker oriented, *sogo shosha* are supply-demand oriented; and unlike merchant banks, who are primarily in the business of handling funds, *sogo shosha* extend credit, make loans, and purchase equity for the sole purpose of stimulating and supporting trade flows.

Today, it is generally acknowledged that the Japanese trading companies classified as *sogo shosha* include such companies as Mitsubishi Corporation, Mitsui & Co., Ltd., C. Itoh and Co., Ltd., Marubeni Corporation, Sumitomo Corporation, Nissho-Iwai, Tomen Ltd., Kanematsu-Cosho and Nichimen. All of these "Big Nine" companies are actively operating in the U.S. today, but Americans are generally unfamiliar with them and the role they play in U.S. export trade. For instance, Americans are often surprised to learn that Mitsui ranks among the leading five exporters of U.S. goods, and that the "Big Nine" account for a $4 billion export surplus for the U.S. in trade with Japan.

ABOUT THE AUTHOR

A.E. Klauser is senior vice-president and executive assistant to the president of Mitsui & Co. (U.S.A.) Inc., and is in charge of Mitsui's office in Washington, D.C.

Mr. Klauser has spent over 15 years in Japan with the U.S. government, with AMF as director of the Far East, and with Pfizer International as general manager for consumer products in the Far East.

He has written articles on U.S./Japanese management and business for *The Journal* of the American Chamber of Commerce.

Mr. Klauser received a Japanese Language Certificate from the University of Chicago and his B.A. and M.A. degrees from the University of Michigan, where he did work on his doctorate in Chinese and Japanese studies. He received his J.D. from Yale University Law School.

ORIGINS OF JAPANESE TRADING COMPANIES

The history of modern Japanese trading companies begins in 1868 with the overthrow of the feudal Tokugawa regime and its replacement by the new government of Emperor Meiji. Ten years before, Japan's 200-year period of isolation had been forcibly ended by the Western maritime powers, who, at the time, were subjugating and colonizing most of Asia. These events caused Japan's leaders to realize that a similar fate faced them, unless political and economic equality with the West could be quickly achieved. As a result, the old imperial government was restored, but dedicated to a new approach and goal: modernizing Japan's political, social, and economic framework, using Western models.

The acquisition of Western know-how and technology combined with the rapid industrialization of the country was essential to the new government's development plan. The Meiji government took the lead in supporting and developing former feudal industries and starting new strategic industries, including mining, shipbuilding, railroads, telegraph, textiles, machine tools, cement, glass, and the like.

In the 1870s, the government entreated and encouraged private capital to participate in the reindustrialization effort. It approached traditional merchant families, such as Mitsui and Sumitomo, as well as enterprising Samurai businessmen, like Yataro Iwasaki, founder of Mitsubishi, and offered them the government's mines, shipyards, and pilot factories at ridiculously low prices.

Some of these families and individuals accepted the challenge and were successful. They organized vertical and horizontal combinations of companies, including banking, manufacturing, and marketing. Control of these conglomorates, *zaibatsu*, reposed in owner families through family holding companies. Some of the combines concentrated on one or a few sectors (textiles, metals, or mining); others, like Mitsui and Mitsubishi, expanded to include a variety of industries and activities.

To provide the nation's newly developing industries with the critical raw materials and technology needed, trading companies developed. They were not only essential for procuring, importing, and distributing the foreign essentials, but also important for obtaining hard currency by exporting local production.

In its first three years (1876–79), Mitsui had opened overseas branches in Shanghai, London, and New York. Other combines quickly developed their trading arms, and in less than 50 years they were handling 80 percent of Japan's total trade. While some *zaibatsu* combines failed or merged with others, they generally expanded but continued to specialize in one or two industrial sectors. The two largest, Mitsui and Mitsubishi, however, branched out into a variety of industries. According to former Ambassador Edwin Reischauer, their growth in the 1920s and 1930s was so enormous that they probably constituted the world's two largest private economic empires.[2] The term *sogo shosha* was first used to describe them.

POST WORLD WAR II DEVELOPMENT OF THE SOGO SOSHA

Following World War II, the Allied Occupation Powers, operating on the theory that the *zaibatsu* had been the cause of Japan's military expansionism, dissolved the *zaibatsu* holding companies, removed top *zaibatsu* officers, and began dismantling the combines. Thus both *sogo shosha* and *senmon shosha* connected with *zaibatsu* were terminated. However, this reform policy was shortly thereafter halted and replaced by a policy fostering Japan's economic recovery.

Although ownership of the *zaibatsu* was not restored to the family holding companies, ex-*zaibatsu* managers were reinstated and allowed, even encouraged, to reconstitute their fragmented industrial group companies. The policy to resurrect Japan's industry was given added emphasis by the outbreak of the Korean War in 1950, and Japan was developed as a giant supply base.

As they had 75 years earlier, the Japanese government was to depend heavily on its re-formed trading companies to rebuild its economy and industrial structure, as well as to provide material for the Korean War effort. From the late 1940s until the mid-1950, Mitsui and Mitsubishi reestablished their general trading company functions, along with many of their other companies within their respective groups. The trading companies of the more specialized former *zaibatsu* groups also re-formed, but broadened their activities to meet the expanded economic needs of the country. To withstand the radical fluctuations of the Japanese economy during the postwar years, some of these companies merged to survive. Thus, by the mid-1960s, 13 *sogo shosha* emerged.[3] As a result of several subsequent mergers and one failure, this number was reduced to today's "Big Nine."

Perhaps we can say that Japan's environment and the unique circumstances and events surrounding it were particularly suitable for developing their *sogo shosha*. In both cases (following the Meiji Restoration and for 15 years after WWII), Japan was comparatively isolated and free from external interference. In addition, the homogeneity of its society helped to synchronize individual expectations with national goals, and government and business were able to cooperate to the mutual benefit of the national economy and the private sector.

Unlike Japan, the U.S. has not sought to stimulate the formation of its own ETCs for a first-stage rebuilding of a new economy. Rather, our government now supports their development in order to improve our economy by enhancing U.S. export efforts.

Although our environment, conditions, and needs are dissimilar to

Japan's, this does not mean that the introduction and use of ETCs at this time is infeasible or unrealistic. The world's increasing economic and commercial interdependence is forcing the U.S. to become more actively engaged in international trade. While our new ETCs may never become carbon copies of the *sogo shosha*, the very attention and effort they are being given by government and business constitute an excellent first step for focusing the attention of American enterprise on foreign trade. Indeed, these ETCs can become catalysts for closer government and business cooperation in the continued development of a viable U.S. foreign trade effort and policy.

JAPANESE MODELS, AMERICAN RESPONSES

Let's take a closer look at some of the key elements that characterize the way *sogo shosha* operate. Although we cannot emulate certain features of these Japanese companies, we may be able to learn some valuable lessons from them.

Size of the Sogo Shosha

The "Big Nine" maintain over 1,000 overseas offices plus 365 in Japan, and their combined annual transactions top $350 billion. Mitsui, for example, has 153 overseas branches in 88 countries and 49 offices in Japan. Its U.S. subsidiary, Mitsui and Co. (U.S.A.), Inc., has 16 branches in the United States with annual trading transactions of over $11 billion.

If the size of these *sogo shosha* seems awesome, remember that they have had the benefit of more than 100 years of active international trading experience. This has enabled them to develop large, highly sophisticated international organizations and trade networks.

The American Response

Except for a few trading companies (such as Cargill and Phibro-Solomon, which deal primarily in grain, metals, and coal), the U.S. does not have any huge, diversified trading companies. The recently established subsidiaries of large U.S. multinational firms, such as Sears and General Electric, however, may have this potential.

But size, in itself, may not be essential if the trading objective is to target a particular country or region or to concentrate on a particular line of products or services. The ETC Act provides American enterprises and banks with a new freedom for collective, horizontal, and vertical integration. Companies intending to export can pool their individual capabilities and overseas networks; they can share risk, gain access to credit through bank participation, and enjoy economies of scale.

Range of Products Handled and Services Provided

Speaking before the Foreign Correspondents Club of Japan in February of last year, Mr. Yohei Mimura, the president of Mitsubishi Shoji Kaisha, Ltd., metaphorically described the role of a *sogo shosha* by using a bowl of shrimp-fried soup, called "tempura soba." He began by explaining all the ingredients that make up this traditional soup: Canadian buckwheat flour for the noodles, U.S. soybeans for the sauce and frying oil, Indonesian shrimp, and U.S. wheat flour for the batter. Moreover, liquified natural gas from Brunei was used for boiling and cooking. "If you trace the flow of these ingredients from foreign and domestic sources," Mimura said, "you have the microcosm of an integrated trader."

Mr. Mimura's point was well made. These large traders are involved in and coordinate the location, purchase, shipping, insuring, financing, and distribution of a great number of items. Mitsui, for example, handles literally everything from soup to nuts—Campbell soups to California almonds. Included among the more than 20,000 different items are general merchandise, commodities, ferrous and nonferrous metals, petrochemicals, electronics, machinery, nuclear generators, tractors, turn-key industrial plants, and engineering and construction services. To facilitate the smooth, expeditious movement and handling of these goods and services, the large trading companies offer a full range of integrated business and service activities.

The American Response

Again, the U.S. still has nothing comparable to the *sogo shosha* with respect to their size and the diversity and volume of the goods handled and the services provided. This fact, however, should not discourage our ETCs. It may be neither necessary nor in their best interests to attempt such ambitious efforts, at least initially. By concentrating on several products and on one or several market areas, these ETCs *can* do an effective and highly competitive job. Whatever supporting trade service may be required (transportation, communication, financing, and the like) can be secured by combining other companies in the ETC.

Profitability and Financial Performance

At first glance (and by U.S. standards), it would seem that *sogo shosha* are not very profitable: Their average gross trading profit is only about 2 percent of their trading transactions. However, when we look at the enormous volume of business transacted, and at the relatively low capital-to-sales ratios, we can appreciate their strategy for maintaining profitability. These companies are interested in long-term, continuous business, in increased trade flows, and in new business along the way, rather than in quick-return bonanzas.

Historically, *sogo shosha* enjoy strong ties with financial institutions, including banks. And the extremely high rate at which their capital is turned over each year allows them to maintain a fairly liquid position.

Although *sogo shosha* are seeing increases in both domestic and foreign trade, the latter is growing more rapidly. These trading companies are expanding their investment in foreign joint ventures, and many have organized consortia to invest and participate in Third World countries for resource development and infrastructure support projects. Again, this is part of a medium- to long-range investment strategy aimed at maintaining and generating new sources of supply and new business.

The American Response

American companies that plan to enter international trade may have to shift their profit objectives and investment strategies from short to long term. Success in foreign trade is based on longer term, continuing business relations, not short-term deals to make quick profits.

American ETCs may need to put greater emphasis on generating profit in other ways: by maximizing plant or service capacity utilization, for example, or by achieving greater economies of scale.

FOUR CRITICAL AREAS

What makes the *sogo shosha* successful? It's not just their immense size and global coverage, nor the scope and diversity of the goods and services handled. What is important is that these companies have acquired and developed experienced professionals and finely tuned management systems to provide a coordinated and integrated "one stop" service. Four areas are considered integral and crucial.

1. Transportation. Quick, on-schedule delivery of orders is absolutely essential for international competitiveness. Transportation includes not only shipping, but rate and scheduling expertise, packaging, insuring, warehousing, loading and unloading, customs clearance, and distribution. Mitsui considered transportation so vital that it became the first trading house to own its own shipping line. Similarly, through joint ventures and affiliated companies, Mitsui owns or controls many of its own transportation channels, warehouses, granaries, freight terminals, loading and unloading facilities, packing and container companies and insurance companies in many foreign countries as well as in Japan.

Developing such effective and highly coordinated transportation facilities and operations could be a problem for some new ETCs. However, these ETCs can acquire such capabilities by combining with a railroad or trucking line, with a freight forwarder or a port authority, or with a large export management company or a multinational trading firm.

2. Communications and Information. An ability to provide rapid and accurate information covering a wide range of subjects is the lifeblood of *sogo shosha* operations. Such information alerts customers to emerging market opportunities and foreign exchange rate fluctuations as well as providing timely economic and political risk information. Using its global communications network, a trading company may exchange over 80,000 messages daily, with each message received within minutes of the time it is fed into the computer.

American ETCs can avoid the enormous capital investment required to establish such networks by combining with city or regional banks or multinational companies that already have overseas offices, or by leasing these services from the American branches of *sogo shosha*.

3. Financial and credit services. Given today's increasingly competitive international marketplace, one of the great strengths of the *sogo shosha* is their close working relationships with banks and other financial and governmental institutions, which give them ready access to loans at very favorable rates. *Sogo shosha* can obtain large loans from these financial institutions, which they then use to extend trade credits and financing to their clients at the trading companies' own risk. In essence, the *sogo shosha* act as intermediaries between these financial organizations and smaller customers who might otherwise have difficulty obtaining direct bank financing.

Considerable foreign trade is won or lost on the credit terms offered, and for this reason it may be important for smaller ETCs to consider having a bank or other financial institution participate in their operations.

4. International trading and management expertise. Without their thousands of dedicated, highly trained, international managers and traders, *sogo shosha* could not function. From the time they graduate from Japan's top universities and enter the company, these individuals are trained to understand all aspects of international trade and commerce. Rather than simply responding to demand in the market, *shosha* executives have an activist approach ingrained in them. They know how to trade and invest, how to seek out and even *create* demand, and how to find innovative ways to effectively supply it. They become trade-flow problem solvers and focus on devising the most expeditious use of technical and human resources to serve clients and stimulate new business. Many of these professionals speak several languages and are often assigned abroad to study and work. *Shosha* executives quite literally devote their entire careers to becoming specialists in international trade.

It is in this area of international trading and management experience that our new ETCs may be found most inadequate. Our current educational system and American business culture produces few truly global-thinking, international managers equipped with the requisite skills and breadth of international trading experience to participate competitively in foreign trade.

It will take time to develop a cadre of international traders. New ETCs may have to rely on the expertise of others, such as international banks, multinational corporations, and multinational trading firms.

WILL THE NEW ETCs SERVE AS A SPEARHEAD IN AMERICA'S EXPORT EFFORT?

Our nation faces a major challenge to end its preoccupation with the domestic marketplace and actively engage in international trade. It is too early to tell whether the new ETCs will constitute effective vehicles for this purpose. If nothing more, the passage of the ETC Act and the national effort being given to promote it emphasize the country's recognition of the importance of international trade to our economic recovery. With the government's continuing encouragement and support, and through the relaxation of antitrust and banking regulations for enterprises primarily engaged in export, a new dimension in trading opportunities is possible.

The U.S. Commerce Department's International Trade Administration now provides information on ETCs and contact facilitation service in 48 of its district offices throughout the country. American branches of sogo shosha, as well, are willing to provide advice to would-be participants. For them, the more companies that become interested in export, the greater the trade-flows—and the larger the international trade pie for everyone. While we can look at these sogo shosha as competitors, we should also consider them as potential partners.

Indeed, with strong, constant government support, together with the effective pooling of our business and banking resources and the ample application of American entrepreneurship, our ETCs can spearhead the opening of a new era for America in this vast new arena.

REFERENCES

1. Yoshio Tsurumi, Sogo Shosha: Engines of Export-Based Growth (Montreal: The Institute for Research on Public Policy, 1980), p. 3.
2. J.K. Fairbank, E.O. Reischauer, and A.M. Craig, A History of East Asian Civilization (Boston: Houghton Mifflin, 1965), Vol. II, p. 506.
3. Yoshio Tsurumi, Sogo Shosha, pp. 20–22.

Appendix A

LIST OF SUBJECTS IN 12 C.F.R. PART 211

Banks, banking; Federal Reserve System; foreign banking; investments; reporting requirements.

Pursuant to its authority under section 5 of the Bank Holding Company Act (12 U.S.C. § 1844), the Board proposes to amend 12 C.F.R. Part 211 by adding a new Subpart C, reading as follows:

Subpart C: Export Trading Companies
Section 211.31: Authority, Purpose and Scope

(a) *Authority.* This Subpart is issued by the Board of Governors of the Federal Reserve System ("Board") under the authority of the Bank Holding Company Act of 1956, as amended (12 U.S.C. § 1841 *et seq.*) ("BHC Act"), and the Bank Export Services Act (Title II, Pub. L. 97-290, 96 Stat. 1235 (1982)) ("BESA").

(b) *Purpose and Scope.* This Subpart is in furtherance of the purposes of the BHC Act and the BESA, the latter statute being designed to increase U.S. exports by encouraging investments and participation in export trading companies by bank holding companies and the specified investors. The provisions of this Subpart apply to: (1) bank holding companies as defined in section 2 of the BHC Act (12 U.S.C. § 1841(a)); (2) Edge and Agreement corporations, as described in section 211.1(b) of this Part, that are subsidiaries of bank holding companies but are not subsidiaries of banks; (3) bankers' banks as described in section 4(c)(14) (F)(iii) of the BHC Act (12 U.S.C. § 1843(c)(14)(F)(iii)); and (4) foreign banking organizations as defined in section 211.23(a)(2) of this Part. These entities are hereinafter referred to as "eligible investors."

Section 211.32: Definitions

The definitions of section 211.2 in Subpart A apply to this Subpart subject to the following:

(a) "Export trading company" means a company that is exclusively engaged in activities related to international trade and, by engaging in one or more export trade services, derives more than one-half its revenues in each consecutive two-year period from the export of, or from facilitating the export of, goods and services produced in the United States by persons other than the export trading company or its subsidiaries. For purposes of this subsection, revenues shall include net sales revenues from exporting, importing, or third party trade in goods by the export trading company for its own account and gross revenues derived from all other activities of the export trading company.

(b) The terms "bank," "company" and "subsidiary" have the same meanings as those contained in section 2 of the BHC Act (12 U.S.C. § 1841).

Section 211.33: Investments and Extensions of Credit

(a) *Amount of Investments.* In accordance with the procedures of section 211.34 of this Subpart, an eligible investor may invest no more than five per cent of its consolidated capital and surplus in one or more export trading companies, except that an Edge or Agreement corporation not engaged in banking may invest as much as 25 per cent of its consolidated capital and surplus but no more than five per cent of the consolidated capital and surplus of its parent bank holding company.

(b) *Extensions of credit.*

(1) *Amount.* An eligible investor in an export trading company or companies may extend credit directly or indirectly to the export trading company or companies in a total amount that at no time exceeds 10 per cent of the investor's consolidated capital and surplus.

(2) *Terms.* An eligible investor in an export trading company may not extend credit directly or indirectly to the export trading company or any of its customers or to any other investor holding 10 per cent or more of the shares of the export trading company on terms more favorable than those afforded similar borrowers in similar circumstances, and such extensions of credit shall not involve more than the normal risk of repayment or present other unfavorable features. For

the purposes of this provision, an investor in an export trading company includes any affiliate of the investor.

(3) *Collateral requirements.* Covered transactions between a bank and an affiliated export trading company in which a bank holding company has invested pursuant to this Subpart are subject to the collateral requirements of section 23A of the Federal Reserve Act (12 U.S.C. § 371c), except where a bank issues a letter of credit or advances funds to an affiliated export trading company solely to finance the purchase of goods for which: (i) the export trading company has a bona fide contract for the subsequent sale of the goods; and (ii) the bank has a security interest in the goods or in the proceeds from their sale at least equal in value to the letter of credit or the advance.

Section 211.34: Procedures for Filing and Processing Notices

(a) *Filing notice.*

(1) *Prior notice of investment.* An eligible investor shall give the Board 60 days' prior written notice of any investment in an export trading company.

(2) *Subsequent notice.* An eligible investor shall give the Board 60 days' prior written notice of changes in the activities of an export trading company that is a subsidiary of the investor if the export trading company expands its activities beyond those described in the initial notice to include: (i) taking title to goods; (ii) product research and design; (iii) product modification; or (iv) activities not specifically covered by the list of services contained in section 4(c)(14)(F)(ii) of the BHC Act. Such an expansion of activities shall be regarded as a proposed investment under this Subpart.

(b) *Time period for Board action.*

(1) A proposed investment that has not been disapproved by the Board may be made 60 days after the Reserve Bank accepts the notice for processing. A proposed investment may be made before the expiration of the 60-day period if the Board notifies the investor in writing of its intention not to disapprove the investment.

(2) The Board may extend the 60-day period for an additional 30 days if the Board determines that the investor has not furnished all necessary information or that any material information furnished is substantially inaccurate. The Board may disapprove an investment if

the necessary information is provided within a time insufficient to allow the Board reasonably to consider the information received.

(3) Within three days of a decision to disapprove an investment, the Board shall notify the investor in writing and state the reasons for the disapproval.

By order of the Board of Governors, June 2, 1983.

(signed) William W. Wiles
William W. Wiles
Secretary of the Board

Appendix B

PROCEDURES FOR BANK HOLDING COMPANY NOTIFI-CATION TO FEDERAL RESERVE OF PROPOSED INVEST-MENT IN AN ETC*

This section presents the nuts and bolts of the Federal Reserve procedures that a banking organization must follow when it plans to invest in an export trading company.

Notice to Federal Reserve Bank

Once the notice of proposed investment has been completed, the banking investor should send the original plus eleven copies to the appropriate Federal Reserve Bank in its district. If the Reserve Bank judges the notice to be complete, the 60-day statutory period for review begins. The Reserve Bank then forwards the complete notice to the Federal Reserve Board in Washington. Within two to four weeks, the Reserve Bank also sends the board a memorandum containing its analysis of the notice and the bank's recommendation for board action.

From the outset, the potential investor may find it helpful to confer informally with members of the board or Federal Reserve Bank staff in person or by telephone. Both the Federal Reserve staff and the banking investors have found such conferences to be very useful, especially now, while the ETC industry in the United States is in its initial stages of development. These discussions provide an opportunity for the Federal Reserve staff to give guidance to the investors on how to prepare their notifications and to clear up any potential problems the staff or the

*The editor wishes to express his appreciation to Cary Williams, an attorney with the Legal Division of the Board of Governors of the Federal Reserve System, for supplying material for this section.

board might see in the proposals. All such preliminary discussions can be treated by the staff as off-the-record and confidential.

Board Review

The board generally receives the notice from the Reserve Bank within about a week after the Reserve Bank accepts it. The clearing unit logs in the notice and sends copies of it to the Division of Bank Supervision and Regulation and the Legal Division. The managers of these divisions assign the notice to analysts and attorneys, respectively. If the notice raises any noteworthy issues, representatives of the appropriate divisions responsible for the matter—such as International Finance or Legal and Bank Supervision and Regulation—hold meetings to discuss those issues.

Next, the board staff makes its recommendations regarding action the board should take on the notice. The board considers the staff's recommendations at one of its regularly scheduled meetings, which are normally held every Monday and Wednesday. Because ETC notices contain confidential business information, they are discussed at a closed meeting. If the notice involves no novel or controversial issue, it may be put on the "Summary Agenda," in which case it will be discussed only if a board member specifically requests discussion. Within three days of board action, a letter will be sent to the applicant, advising it of the board's decision. In addition, the board staff will call the applicant to inform it of the board's decision.

Once the notice is approved, the banking investor is free to proceed with its plans. The investment must be made within one year from the date of the letter of approval, unless the board or the Reserve Bank extends the time. The investor should advise the Reserve Bank in writing within ten days of consummation of the transaction. The investor also must give the board 60 days' prior written notice of certain changes in the activities of an ETC, if they include, for example, taking title to goods, product modification, and the like. (See § 211.34(a) (2) of the Board's regulations). Otherwise, at this time, the board requires no special reporting by the investor of its ETC activities, but only those reports already required of the banking organization investors.

Appendix C

CERTIFICATE OF REVIEW APPLICATION PROCESS—U.S. DEPARTMENT OF COMMERCE

Application Procedure

Before counseling with the Office of Export Trading Company Affairs (OETCA), applicants should first read through the ETC Act, its guidelines and regulations. Preliminary discussions with the OETCA's staff attorneys and antitrust economists can provide applicants with valuable information about the ETC program. Applicants should bring an outline of their business plans with them to the counseling session.

The OETCA will accept "draft" applications, thus giving applicants a chance to proceed through a "dry run." This can alleviate the problem of supplying insufficient data during the real application process.

Formal Application

1. Applicants should submit one completed application, along with three copies.

2. An application must be reviewed for completeness by the OETCA within 5 working days after it is received. At that time, it must be accepted as complete or returned to the applicant. If OETCA does not respond in 5 days, the application is deemed submitted.

3. The OETCA will forward one copy to the Department of Justice not later than 7 days after the application is deemed complete.

4. Should a request for expedited review be granted by both the OETCA and the Department of Justice, the application must then be processed within 45 days, but no sooner than 30 days after the date on which it was accepted as complete.

5. Within 10 days after the application has been accepted, the OETCA must transmit for publication in the Federal Register a summary of the applicant's proposed activities.

6. On day 70 after the application is accepted, the OETCA must forward a "draft" certificate to the Department of Justice.

7. On day 90, the OETCA, with the concurrence of the Department of Justice, must either issue or deny a certificate to the applicant.